# THE ANTHROPOSOPHIC MOVEMENT

CW01455798

# THE ANTHROPOSOPHIC MOVEMENT

THE HISTORY AND CONDITIONS OF THE
ANTHROPOSOPHICAL MOVEMENT IN RELATION TO
THE ANTHROPOSOPHICAL SOCIETY

*An Encouragement For Self-Examination*

Eight lectures given in Dornach from 10 to 17 June 1923

TRANSLATED AND INTRODUCED
BY CHRISTIAN VON ARNIM

## RUDOLF STEINER

RUDOLF STEINER PRESS

CW 258

Rudolf Steiner Press
Hillside House, The Square
Forest Row, RH18 5ES
www.rudolfsteinerpress.com

Published by Rudolf Steiner Press 2022

Originally published in German under the title *Die Geschichte und die Bedingungen der anthroposophischen Bewegung im Verhältnis zur Anthroposophischen Gesellschaft. Eine Anregung zur Selbstbesinnung* (volume 258 in the *Rudolf Steiner Gesamtausgabe* or Collected Works) by Rudolf Steiner Verlag, Dornach. Based on shorthand notes that were not reviewed or revised by the speaker. This authorized translation is based on the third German edition (1981), edited by Dr H. W. Zbinden

Published by permission of the Rudolf Steiner Nachlassverwaltung, Dornach

© Rudolf Steiner Nachlassverwaltung, Dornach, Rudolf Steiner Verlag 1981

This translation © Rudolf Steiner Press 2022

All rights reserved. No part of this publication may be reproduced, stored in a retrieval system, or transmitted, in any form or by any means, electronic, mechanical, photocopying or otherwise, without the prior permission of the publishers

A catalogue record for this book is available from the British Library

ISBN 978 1 85584 603 6

Cover by Morgan Creative
Typeset by Symbiosys Technologies, Vishakapatnam, India
Printed and bound by 4Edge Ltd., Essex

# CONTENTS

# Publisher's Note

T HE present lectures for members of June 1923 are the result of Rudolf Steiner's endeavour to steer the Anthroposophical Society towards a reconsideration of the actual foundations of anthroposophy and the inner conditions for working on the tasks of the time. After the War, the Society had become increasingly fragmented into external individual initiatives and practical projects. Although Rudolf Steiner had been speaking words of warning since 1921, and at the end of 1922 had called on leading personalities to make proposals for it to be newly consolidated, it was not until the catastrophic fire to which the first Goetheanum fell victim on New Year's Eve 1922/23 that a new direction emerged. Individual national societies were founded in the course of 1923. (See *Das Schicksalsjahr 1923 in der Geschichte der Anthroposophischen Gesellschaft*, GA 259, as well as *Awakening to Community*, CW 257.) On 10 June, immediately before the first lecture of the present volume, it was decided at the Annual General Meeting of the Anthroposophical Society in Switzerland—acting on a proposal from the Society in Great Britain—to hold a meeting of delegates from all countries at the end of July which was to produce measures for the reconstruction of the Goetheanum. This international meeting of delegates, from 20 to 23 July, led to the decision to unite the individual national societies at Christmas 1923 into an international Anthroposophical Society based at the Goetheanum. Its leadership was to be assumed by a General Secretary to be elected at that time. Shortly before Christmas, however, Rudolf Steiner decided to take this position on himself (see further in *The Christmas Conference for the Foundation of the General Anthroposophical Society 1923/24*, CW 260).

# INTRODUCTION

T HE history of the Anthroposophical Society and the anthroposophical movement has not always been easy or smooth.

On the one hand, the period starting in about 1910—shortly
before the split with the Theosophical Society and the founding
of the Anthroposophical Society—through to the early 1920s was
a very productive time. Construction of the first Goetheanum in
Switzerland as the international centre for anthroposophy started in
1913. Workers and artists from all over Europe were involved in the
building work, which continued throughout the First World War.

A year earlier, in 1912, Rudolf Steiner had begun to develop the
new movement art of eurythmy. Then, in the years after the War, the
first Waldorf school was founded in 1919; Steiner and the physician
Ita Wegman established anthroposophical medicine in 1921, not as a
replacement for conventional medicine but to extend it as a system
of complementary and integrative medicine; biodynamic agriculture
had its beginning in a course of lectures at Whitsun 1924, to name
but some of the developments in which, with the anthroposophical
movement, Steiner sought to fertilize the life of society in education,
the arts, science, the economy and social affairs.

But alongside these initiatives the Anthroposophical Society had
increasingly fractured after the War, including differences between
younger and older members, and lost its sense of purpose, something Rudolf Steiner had warned about since 1921, ultimately leading
to the foundation of a new society at Christmas 1923. In an attempt
to guide members of the Anthroposophical Society to reflect on the
real foundations of anthroposophy in the context of the anthroposophical movement at this critical stage in its development, in these
lectures in June 1923 Steiner comprehensively reviewed and set out

the way anthroposophy had evolved from its beginnings. But he also urged members to reflect on the kind of attitudes required in a society that sought to represent a true spiritual outlook on and insights into life.

Rudolf Steiner uses as his reference point throughout these lectures what he calls the 'homeless souls' seeking to find the spirit in a social setting of conventions and traditions which had outlived their time and in which a materialistic outlook predominated. The Theosophical Society seemed to offer these souls a home and so in the lectures Steiner spends a lot of time looking at where things went wrong in the Theosophical Society, as if wanting to illustrate how *not* to conduct life in a society that wished to offer a true home to those souls seeking real access to the spirit; he comments, for example, on the lack of real spiritual knowledge among the people lecturing there, merely repeating what he called old rehashed theories in ancient writings. He nevertheless gives a very nuanced appraisal of H. P. Blavatsky and her writings.

Steiner is keen to emphasize that anthroposophy and the Anthroposophical Society are not an offshoot of the Theosophical Society but that anthroposophy as developed by him ploughed its own furrow from the beginning—even when it had not yet been given that name. He argues that in bringing his spiritual insights he had to start at the place people—the homeless souls looking for spiritual knowledge—were, and that at the time the Theosophical Society offered the best vehicle for that since it was also the place to which many of them were drawn in their search. As he put it, anthroposophy did not need to concern itself with the answers the Theosophical Society gave to those homeless souls but with the questions they were asking.

Where he feels the Anthroposophical Society could learn from the Theosophical Society, however, is in the consciousness of itself as a society which the latter had developed. The former should develop a similar sense of itself as a society but guided by the ideal that wisdom can only be found in truth—something he found lacking in the Theosophical Society.

When Steiner speaks about the Anthroposophical Society, it is clear that he had great concerns about what it was becoming. What shines through his words, particularly in the last two lectures, is his worry that the Anthroposophical Society had become narrow-minded and exclusionary in its outlook and lacking generosity. He describes being approached by people asking whether they would be able to join the Society since they could not yet profess to the prescriptions of anthroposophy, and he found it terrible that anyone interested in anthroposophy should be made to feel like that. Honest membership should require only one thing, he says, an interest in a society that in general terms seeks the path to the spiritual world. Worse, such an attitude created a view of the Society as being sectarian. What is the use of claiming that it is not a sect when it behaves like one, he asks, presenting itself to the world as holding collective opinions to which members have to subscribe, laying down rules and dictating that things must be done in specific ways.

The lectures end both with a warning and an appeal: The warning that the anthroposophical movement cannot exist in an Anthroposophical Society that consists of cliques and exclusionary groups. (Unless the being of anthroposophy is alive in the Society, it will not thrive and ultimately it will collapse.) And the appeal for his listeners to reflect on his words and develop the kind of self-awareness that will make the continued existence of the Society possible.

*Christian von Arnim*
*September 2022*

# LECTURE ONE

T HE reflections we are embarking on here are intended to encourage a kind of self-examination by all those who have found their way to anthroposophy. An opportunity will be provided for such self-examination, for self-examination brought about by a characterization of the anthroposophical movement and its relationship with the Anthroposophical Society. And in this context may I begin by speaking about the people who are central to such self-examination. They are yourselves. They are all those who, for one reason or another, have found their way to anthroposophy.

Some have found this path through an inner necessity of the soul, an inner necessity of the heart; others, perhaps, found it through the search for knowledge. There are many, however, who entered the anthroposophical movement to a greater or lesser extent for outer reasons and then perhaps found more in this anthroposophical movement through a deepening of the soul than they at first thought. But there is one characteristic which all those who find their way to the anthroposophical movement have in common. And if we draw together from the various years what is characteristic of those who find their way into the anthroposophical movement, then we have to say that ultimately they are driven initially by their inner destiny, their karma, to leave the ordinary highway of civilization on which the majority of humanity at present progresses to search for their own path.

Let us consider for a moment the conditions in which most people grow into life from childhood in our age. They are born to parents who are French or German, Catholic or Protestant or Jewish, or who belong to some other faith. They might be born to parents who hold a variety of opinions. But there is always a kind of unquestioned assumption when people are born in the present time, in the first instance among the parents, the members of the family into which these people are born from out of their pre-earthly existence. It is what we might call the unquestioned assumption—which remains unspoken and which is felt without perhaps being thought about, although often it is also thought about when there is reason to do so—that people look at life in general and naturally think: We are French and Catholic or German and Protestant and our children will most likely become the same.

These kinds of feelings naturally engender a social ambience, indeed social pressures, which more or less clearly, or indeed unclearly, push children into the kind of life which has been mapped out by these feelings, these more or less clearly defined thoughts. To begin with, then, the life of a child follows its natural course of education and schooling. And during this time parents once again have all kinds of thoughts which again are not expressed but which are a decisive prerequisite for life, which exercise an exceptional influence on life. The thought, for instance, that my son will, of course, enter the secure employment of the civil service; or my son will inherit the parental business; or my daughter will marry the man next door.

Well, it isn't always as concrete as this but an orientation is given, a direction is always marked out. The outer life of today is, after all, organized such that this outer life does indeed obey the impulses that are created in this way, even into our chaotic times to which people for the most part are, however, unaccustomed. And the result is that a person becomes in some way, well, let us say, a French Catholic or a German Protestant. They have to, for that is how the impulses of life take effect. Even if it does not come from the parents with such finality, school life or the circumstances of adolescence, of childhood in general, capture the human being and places them in a given position in life. The state, the religious community draw the person in.

If the majority of people were asked to explain how they got where they are today, they would not be able to do so, because there would be something unbearable about having to think deeply about such matters. This unbearable element tends to be driven underground into subconscious or unconscious areas of our soul life. At best, it will be dredged up by a psychiatrist when it behaves in a particularly recalcitrant manner down there in those unknown provinces of the soul. But mostly our own personality, the individuality, is simply not strong enough to assert itself against what we have grown into in this way.

Occasionally people have the urge to rebel when their situation as a trainee, or even following qualification, unexpectedly dawns on them. You might clench your fist in your pocket, or, if you are a woman, create a scene at home because of such disappointed expectations of life. These are reactions against what people are forced to become. We also frequently seek to anaesthetize ourselves by concentrating on the pleasant things in life. We go to dances and follow this with a long lie-in, don't we? Time is then filled up in one way or another. Or someone might join a thoroughly patriotic party because their professional position demands that they belong to something which will accept them. We have already been accepted by the state and our religion; now that must be supplemented by surrounding what we have unconsciously grown into with a sort of aura. Well, there is no need for me to go into further detail.

That is roughly the way in which the people who move in the mainstream of life have grown into their existence.

But those who cannot go along with this end up on many possible and impossible byways; people who simply cannot go along with most of the prescribed trajectories of the present find themselves on numerous possible and impossible paths. And anthroposophy is precisely one of these paths on which human beings are seeking what lies within themselves; on which they want to experience this in a more conscious manner, to experience something which is under their control to a certain extent at least. For the most part, people who do not walk along the highways of life tend to be anthroposophists. Be they young or old, in some way or other they are such people. If we investigate further why that should be, we find that this is linked with the spiritual world.

Souls mostly enter earthly life from their pre-earthly existence after having for a long time passed through the state before birth which I have often characterized in lectures. Having relived the course of their lives in the spiritual world after death, human beings enter a region where they become increasingly assimilated into the spiritual world, where their lives consist of working together with the beings of the higher hierarchies, where all their acts are related to this world of substantive spirit. But in this progression between death and a new birth a time arrives when they begin to turn their attention to earth again. For a long time in advance of their birth, human beings unite on a soul level with the generations at the end of which stand the parents who give birth to them—not only as far back as their great-great-grandparents, but much further down the line of preceding generations. The majority of souls nowadays look down, as it were, to earth from the spiritual world and display a lively interest in what is happening to their ancestors.

Now it is the case with the majority of the souls of the present time that in the time in which they are preparing to return to earth they have a burning interest in what is happening on earth. They look down to earth from the spiritual world, as it were, and take a lively interest in what is happening on earth with their forebears. Such souls become as I have just characterized, for those who move in the mainstream of contemporary life.

In contrast, there are a number of souls, particularly at present, whose interest is concentrated less on worldly happenings as they approach earthly existence from pre-earthly existence than on the question of how they can develop maturity in the spiritual world. Their interest lies in the spiritual world right up to the moment at which they find their way to earth.

Whereas the others have a deep desire for earthly existence, these souls have a lively interest in the things that are happening in the spiritual world and as a consequence, when they incarnate, arrive with a consciousness which has its origins in spiritual impulses and which provides less of an inclination towards those impulses that exist as I have described them for those that follow the mainstream. They outgrow the impulses of their surroundings; with their spiritual ambitions they outgrow their surroundings and are thus predestined and prepared to go their own way.

Thus the souls who descend from pre-earthly to earthly existence can be divided into two types. One type, to which the majority of people today still belong, comprises those souls who can make themselves remarkably at home on earth; who feel thoroughly comfortable in their warm nest which so fascinated them long before they came down to earth, even if they do occasionally experience it as unpleasant—but that is only appearance, that is maya; who feel comfortable in this warm nest in which they already had an interest for a long time before they descended to earth.

Other souls, who may pass patiently through childhood—external maya is not always the decisive thing—are less able to make themselves at home, are homeless souls, and grow beyond the warmth of the nest much more than they grow into it. This latter group includes those who are subsequently attracted to the anthroposophical movement. It is therefore clearly predetermined in a certain sense whether or not we are led to anthroposophy.

So we can say: The things which are being sought by these souls on the byways of life, away from the major highways, manifest themselves in many ways. Anyone who has experienced life with a certain awareness in the last decades of the nineteenth century, in the first decades of the twentieth century, will have found that such homeless souls, especially inwardly homeless souls, appeared everywhere among other people in large numbers, relatively naturally. Many souls today, I would say, have a certain touch of such homelessness.

If the others did not find it so agreeable to take the well-trodden paths and such obstacles were not put in the way of homeless souls, the numbers of the latter would be much more obvious to their contemporaries. But let me say that it is widely apparent today how many souls have a hint of such homelessness about them.

Only very recently it was reported that things such as these are even happening: a professor held a class at a university, announced a semester course on the development—as he called it—of mystical occult ideas from Pythagoras to Steiner, and, after this class was announced, so many people came to the first lecture that he could not speak in an ordinary lecture hall but had to lecture in the main auditorium where usually only the great ceremonial lectures are held.

We can see from such facts how things are today, how indeed the inclination to such homelessness is rooted in souls to an extraordinary extent. It was possible to see all these things asserting themselves today as a longing of souls who carry such homelessness in themselves, growing from week to week; to see it increasingly asserting itself as a longing for a position in life that is not fixed from the outset, directed from the outset; asserting itself more and more as a longing for the spirit from this corner of life, we might say more strongly from week to week in our present chaotic spiritual life—all that could be seen arising. By sketching in outline today how this slowly came about, you can find in this sketch by a kind of self-reflection a little of what I would like to call the anthroposophical origin of all of you. In sketching an outline of this gradual development, you can find in it, if you reflect on it, a little something of what I would like to describe as the anthroposophical origins of each one of you.

By way of introduction today I will do no more than pick out in outline some characteristic features. If you look back at the last decades of the nineteenth century—we could take any number of fields, but let us take a very characteristic one—what might be called Wagnerism, Richard Wagnerism began to take a hold. It is certainly true that much of such Richard Wagnerism consisted of cultural flirtation, sensationalism and so on. But among the people who then appeared when Bayreuth was established, there were not only the gentlemen in the latest fashionable tailcoats and the ladies in the latest fashionable gowns, but there were all kinds of people in Bayreuth. You could see gentlemen with very long hair, ladies with very short hair, you could see people who considered it a kind of modern pilgrimage to come to Bayreuth from far away. I even knew someone who, when he set out for Bayreuth, took off his boots in a very distant place and went barefoot to Bayreuth as a pilgrim.

Among those who came as gentlemen with long hair and ladies with short hair, there were some who somehow belonged to the homeless souls. But even among those who were perhaps not exactly dressed in the latest fashion, but nevertheless in a more respectable fashion, there were those who were also homeless souls.

Now the effect of Wagnerism on people—I speak not only about the musical element but about the movement as a cultural phenomenon—was to offer them something which went beyond all the usual offerings of a materialistic age. It was something which came, I might say was suggested by Wagnerism in particular which gave people a feeling that here there was a gateway to a more spiritual world, a world differing from their normal environment. And on occasion what went on in Bayreuth led to a great longing for more profound spiritual aspirations.

It was, of course, difficult at first to understand Richard Wagner's characters and dramatic compositions. But many people felt that they were created from a source different from the crude materialism of the time. And the homeless souls who were driven in this particular direction were prompted into all kinds of dark, instinctive intuitions through what I might call the suggestive power of Wagnerian drama and specifically through the way of life that it introduced into our culture.

There were, for example, also readers of the *Bayreuther Blätter* among those who found their way into this Wagnerian life. Now it is historically interesting—today all of this is, after all, already history—to take a volume of the *Bayreuther Blätter* and look at how the interpretation of *Tristan and Isolde*, the *Ring of the Nibelungs*, the *Flying Dutchman* is approached; how even the way in which the dramatic design, the individual figures within the Wagner dramas, the processes within them, are approached; and how an attempt is made, albeit in a strongly subjectivizing, unrealistic way, also unrealistic in a spiritual sense, but nevertheless with a spiritual longing, to enter into a more spiritual contemplation of things and of human life in general. Indeed, it is true to say that subsequent interpretations by theosophists of *Hamlet* or other works of art are very strongly reminiscent of certain essays which were written by Hans von Wolzogen, who was not a theosophist but a trained Wagnerian, in the *Bayreuther Blätter*.[1] For example, let's say you woke up one morning and some troll had replaced the theosophical journal that you may have read fifteen years ago with a copy of the *Bayreuther Blätter*, you could really confuse the tone and attitude of the latter with what you found in your theosophical journal, if it was an article by Wolzogen or something similar.

Thus we can say that Wagnerism was the reason why many people, possessed of a homeless soul, became acquainted with a way of looking at the world which led away from crude materialism towards something spiritual; and all those who became part of such a current—not because of a superficial cultural flirtation but because of an inner compulsion of the soul—wanted to develop their experience of a spiritual world because they felt this kind of inner longing. Of them we can indeed say: They were no longer concerned with the certain evidence which underpinned the materialistic worldview. That was true irrespective of their position in life, whether they were lawyers or artists, cabinet ministers, parliamentarians or whatever—even scientists.

As I said, I could also have quoted other areas where such homeless souls can be found. Such homeless souls could be found everywhere. But Wagnerism provides a particularly characteristic example of the presence of very many such souls.

Well, it was then my task to become acquainted subsequently with a number of such souls in a different guise, but once again in the company of others who had, as it were, undergone their spiritual novitiate in Wagnerism. These were souls with whom I became acquainted in Vienna[2] in the late 1880s in a group which consisted of many such homeless souls. People no longer really appreciate the way in which that homelessness was visible for anyone to see even then, because many of the things which at that time required a great deal of inner courage have today become commonplace.

For example, I do not believe that many people today could imagine the following. I was sitting in a circle of such homeless souls and all kinds of things had already been discussed. Then someone arrived later, who had been kept busy for longer than the others, or perhaps had stayed at home, preoccupied with his own thoughts, and started to speak about Dostoevsky's Raskolnikov,[3] spoke about Raskolnikov in such a manner that the group felt as if struck by lightning. A new world opened up: it was like suddenly finding oneself on a new planet. That is how these souls felt.

Allow me to say: in all these observations of life which I am recounting by way of an introduction to the history of the anthroposophical movement, I must mention that in the time that I was compelled by destiny to make such observations of life I never lost my connection with the spiritual world, my location inside the spiritual world. It was always there. I mention this because it is the background against which I speak: the spiritual world as something self-evident, and human beings on earth perceived as images of their real existence as spiritual beings within the spiritual world. I would like to characterize this frame of mind so that you always take it as given as the spiritual background.

Naturally such observation was not cold-blooded but with a warm interest and without wanting to be an observer, just being involved—in all friendliness and kindness and politeness of course. I was involved and came to know these people, not in order to observe them but because that is how life naturally ordered it. At the end of the eighties I got to know such a circle, which incidentally consisted of people from all professions, from all walks of life; they were such homeless souls, and a number of them had moved here from Wagner's region; they were people who had, so to speak, gone through their spiritual novitiate in Wagner's region. The one I told you about, who took off his boots in Vienna and then went barefoot to Bayreuth, was also among them and was indeed a very witty person. I actually met these personalities quite often for a while, sometimes every day. Having passed through their Wagnerian metamorphosis, they lived in a second metamorphosis.

For example, there were among them three good acquaintances, intimate friends even, of HP Blavatsky,[4] who were keen theosophists in the way that theosophists were when Blavatsky was still alive. But a peculiar quality adhered to theosophists at that time, the period following the appearance of Blavatsky's *Isis Unveiled* and *The Secret Doctrine*. They all had a desire to be extremely esoteric. They had nothing but contempt for their normal life, had nothing but contempt, of course, for their work. The exoteric life, however, was not something which could be avoided. That was a given. But everything else was esoteric. In that setting you spoke only to fellow

initiates, only within a small group. And those who were not considered worthy of talking to about such things were seen as people
with whom they spoke about the ordinary things in life. It was with
the former that you discussed esoteric matters. They were readers,
good readers of Sinnett's *Esoteric Buddhism*[5] which had just been
published at the time, but all of them were people who pre-emi-
nently belonged to the homeless souls I just described; people who,
although they might be engineers from the moment they stepped
into practical life, would with great involvement and the most lively
interest read a book like Sinnett's *Esoteric Buddhism*. These people
possessed a certain urge—partly still as a result of their Wagnerian past—to explain from an esoteric perspective, as they called it,
everything which existed by way of myths.

But as more and more of these homeless souls began to reveal
themselves at the end of the nineteenth century, it was possible to see how the most interesting among them were not those
who studied the writings of Sinnett and Blavatsky—with, let me
say, just a nine-tenths honest mind, at most a nine-tenths honest
mind—but those who did not wish to engage in the reading for
themselves because there were still great inhibitions about such
things at that time, and who listened with gaping mouths when
those who had done the reading expounded on these things. And it
was most interesting to observe how the listeners, who were sometimes more honest than the narrators, grasped these ideas with
their homeless souls as essential spiritual nourishment; spiritual
nourishment which they were able to transform into something
more honest through the greater honesty of their souls, despite
the relative dishonesty with which it was being presented to them.
One could see in them the yearning to hear something completely
different from what was offered in the ordinary cultural mainstream. How they devoured what they heard! It was most interesting to observe how on the one hand the tentacles of mainstream
life kept drawing people in; and how on the other they would then
appear at one of the meeting places—often a coffee house—and
would listen with great yearning to what someone else had in turn
read in one of the newly published books of this kind and who

sometimes laid on quite thickly what they had read. The point is that the honest souls, the ones who had been subject to the vagaries of life, were there too.

The way in which souls not quite willing to admit to their homelessness were unable to find their bearings was particularly evident towards the latter part of the nineteenth century. A person might, for instance, listen with profound interest to an explanation of the physical, etheric and astral bodies, kama manas, manas, buddhi and so on. At the same time they were obliged to write the article their newspaper expected, including all the usual goodies. These people truly became such souls who really showed how difficult it was for some people to leave the mainstream of life specifically at the beginning of the new spiritual development which we have to count as starting at the end of the nineteenth century. For there were several among them who behaved as if they wanted to slink away, and would prefer that no one knew where they had gone when they wished to attend what was most important and interesting to them in life. It was indeed interesting how spiritual life, the wish for something spiritual, the yearning for a spiritual world began particularly to establish itself in European culture.

Now you have to remember that circumstances in the late 1880s were really much more difficult than today. Even if it was less harmful, it was nevertheless more difficult then to admit to the existence of a spiritual world because the physical world of the senses with all its magnificent laws was proven of course! There was no way of getting round that! All the proofs were there in the physics laboratories and the hospitals; all the evidence declared in favour of a world for which there was proof. But the world which could be proven was so unsatisfactory for many homeless souls, was useless to the inner soul, to such an extent that many crept away from it. And at the same time as this great contemporary culture was on offer to them not just by the bushel but by the ton, in huge quantities, they took what nips they could from what has to be seen as the flow of the spiritual world into modern culture. It was not at all easy to speak about the spiritual world; a suitable point of entry had to be found.

If I may once again introduce a personal note. I myself had to find a suitable point where I could create a connection—I couldn't simply crash in on our culture with the spiritual world; it needn't be an external reason, it could be something quite honestly inward. Especially in the late 1880s, I linked the points I had to make about the spiritual world, about its more intimate aspects, in many places with Goethe's *Fairy Tale of the Green Snake and the Beautiful Lily*.[6] It was possible to tie in with that because Goethe, after all, was creditable; it was Goethe, after all, wasn't it? If something was used which had been created by no less a person than Goethe, and when it was as obvious as it is in the *Fairy Tale of the Green Snake and the Beautiful Lily* that spiritual impulses had flowed into it, that was something to use as a link. I certainly could not use what was then being peddled as theosophy, what had been garnered from Blavatsky, from Sinnett's *Esoteric Buddhism* and similar books by a group of people who were undeniably ambitious. For someone who wanted to preserve their scientifically schooled thinking in the spiritual world it was simply impossible to find any kind of connection with what was forming as a spiritual atmosphere directly in line with Blavatsky and Sinnett's *Esoteric Buddhism*.

Neither was it easy in another respect. Why was that? Well, Sinnett's *Esoteric Buddhism* was soon recognized as the work of a spiritual dilettante, a compendium of old, badly understood esoteric bits and pieces. But it was less easy to come to terms with a phenomenon of the period such as Blavatsky's *The Secret Doctrine*. For this work did at least reveal in many places that much of its content had its origins in real, powerful impulses from the spiritual world. So that in numerous passages of Blavatsky's *Secret Doctrine* we find the revelation of a spiritual world through a certain personality, which happened to be Blavatsky.

Above all, one thing was particularly noticeable, especially noticeable in the search to which the people who had come into contact with Blavatsky herself or Blavatsky's *Secret Doctrine* in this way had devoted themselves. The book expressed a large number of ancient truths which had been gained through atavistic clairvoyance in prehistorical ages of humankind. It was a kind of reawakening of ancient cultures. People thus encountered in the outside world, not from within themselves, something which could be described as an uncovering of a tremendous wealth of wisdom which humankind had once possessed as something exceptionally illuminating. This was interspersed with unbelievable passages which never ceased to amaze, because the book is a sloppy and dilettantish piece of work as regards any sort of scientific way of thinking, and includes superstitious nonsense and much more. In short, Blavatsky's *Secret Doctrine* is a peculiar book: great truths sit side by side with terrible rubbish. One might almost say that it sums up very well the spiritual phenomena to which those who developed into the homeless souls of the modern age were subjected. I really did meet many such souls at that time. It was possible to see the arrival of these homeless souls on earth.

In the following period in Weimar[7] I was, of course, occupied intensively with other things, although even then there were numerous opportunities to observe such searching souls. For during this time in particular all kinds of people passed through Weimar to visit the Goethe and Schiller Archive—if I may say so, from all over the world. It was possible to become acquainted with the good and bad sides of their souls in a remarkable way as they passed through Weimar. I got to know some strange people, as well as those who were highly cultivated, refined and distinguished. My description of meeting Herman Grimm,[8] for instance, appeared recently in the last-but-one issue of *Das Goetheanum*.[9]

That really was the case with Herman Grimm, at least for my feeling, when he was in Weimar—he came very frequently when he travelled from Berlin to Italy or back, or also otherwise he came to Weimar very often; and for me the feeling thus developed: there is something different about Weimar when he is there from when he is gone again. Herman Grimm was something that explained Weimar in a special way. You had a better understanding of Weimar when Herman Grimm was there.

We need only think of his novel *Unüberwindliche Mächte*[10] to see how Grimm also exhibited a strong drive for spiritual matters. If you read the end of his novel *Unüberwindliche Mächte*, you can see how the spiritual world intermingles with the physical through the soul of a dying person. It is very moving, very magnificent. I have spoken about this in previous lectures.[11]

Of course some strange people also passed through Weimar. There was a Russian state councillor, for example, who was looking for something. No one could discover what he was looking for: it was something or other in the second part of Goethe's *Faust*. Exactly how he hoped to achieve that through the Goethe Archive was impossible to elicit. It was also hard to know what to do to help him. The people in the Goethe Archive would very much have liked to help him. He just kept searching. He was searching for a point in the second part of *Faust* and you couldn't quite figure out what the point was supposed to be. You just kept hearing that he was looking for the point, the point. In the end he was simply left to continue his search. But he was so talkative on this point that when we were having supper in the evening and he came near, we always said among ourselves: Don't look around, the state councillor is doing the rounds. We didn't want to be found by him.

Now next to him sat another very peculiar visitor who was very witty, an American,[12] but who loved to sit on the floor with his legs crossed, who sat in this way on the floor in front of the books—a very peculiar sight. As I said, that also happened, and it was possible to see such cameos of contemporary life in their most distinctive form.

When subsequently I went to Berlin, destiny once again led me into a group of such souls of which I have said that they were homeless souls. And destiny led me so far in, that this group in particular asked me to give the lectures which have now been published in my *Mystics after Modernism*.[13] I have also told in the Preface to *Mystics* how these things came about. They were people who found their way into the Theosophical Society at a somewhat later date than my Viennese acquaintances. They also had a different relationship to what Blavatsky represented. Only a few of them studied Blavatsky's *Secret Doctrine*. But these people, to whom I presented something quite different in my *Mystics*, were well-versed in what Blavatsky's successor, Annie Besant,[14] proclaimed as the theosophical ideas of the time. They were very well versed in this, and I still remember, for example, that I heard a lecture from a member of this group which built on a small book by Annie Besant, in which she for her part divided the human being like this: physical body, etheric body, astral body and so on. I often recall how terribly awful I found this portrayal of the human being in Annie Besant's sense. I had not read anything by Besant. The first thing I heard from her was this lecture given by a lady in connection with Besant's latest brochure. It was something terrible how the individual constitutional elements of the human being were consecutively listed, basically without any inner understanding, without letting them emerge from the totality of the human being.

So I found myself once again in a similar situation to the one in Vienna in the late 1880s, in which it was possible to observe such homeless souls. And as you know already: anthroposophy essentially at first grew up, one might say, together with—not in, but together with—what was there by way of such homeless souls who had initially sought a new home for their souls in theosophy.

I wanted, my dear friends, to take these reflections to this point today. Tomorrow I will continue and try to lead you further in such self-reflection which we have hardly even begun today.

# Lecture Two

## DORNACH, 11 JUNE 1923

WHEN we discuss the history and conditions of life of anthroposophy in relation to the Anthroposophical Society, any such reflections have to take into account two questions which simply arise from this history. I might formulate these two questions in the following way. First, why was it necessary to link the anthroposophical movement to the theosophical movement in the way they were connected? And second, why is it that malicious opponents still equate anthroposophy with theosophy and the Anthroposophical Society with the Theosophical Society, something that basically only happens for external reasons?

The answers to these questions will only become clear from a historical perspective. Yesterday I said that when we talk about the Anthroposophical Society, the first thing of relevance is what the people are like who feel the need to pursue their path through an anthroposophical movement. And I tried yesterday to describe the sense in which the souls who come into contact with anthroposophy in order to satisfy their spiritual yearning are homeless souls in a certain respect. Such homeless souls did indeed exist at the end of the nineteenth and early twentieth century. There were more of them about than is normally suspected, because there were many people who in one way or another tried by various means to develop their more profound human qualities.

We only need to recall that quite apart from the reaction to modern materialism, which subsequently led to various forms of spiritualism, many souls sought to fulfil certain inner needs by reading the work of people like Ralph Waldo Trine[15] and similar writers. They tried, one might say, to compensate for something missing in their human nature; something which they wanted to feel and experience inwardly, but which they could not find on the well-trodden paths of modern culture, which they could find neither in the popular literature or art of a secular age, nor in the traditional religious faiths.

Today, then, I will place before you a number of facts, and will have to leave it to the following lectures to create the links between them. First of all, it will be a matter of bringing certain facts before our souls in an appropriate way.

Among all the people who were searching in this way, be it on a spiritistic path, be it through Ralph Waldorf Trine or others, were those who joined the then existing various branches of the Theosophical Society. And if we ask whether there was something which distinguished those who joined the Theosophical Society in some form from others who became, for example, spiritists or sought to enrich themselves inwardly through Ralph Waldo Trine, then the answer has to be yes. They were significantly different. There was indeed what I might call a special sort of human search present in those who were driven to some form of the Theosophical Society in particular.

We know from the way in which the Theosophical Society developed that it was not unreasonable to assume that the something which people were looking for at the start of our century as anthroposophy was most likely to be understood within the circles then united by theosophy. But we will only be able to throw some light on that if the facts are properly presented.

Now, pausing here, I would first like to characterize the people who came together there, to draw a kind of picture of what could be understood at that time as the Theosophical Society, which found its most succinct expression in the English Theosophical Society. It was followed, after all, by what then emerged as anthroposophy, or rather, what actually immediately emerged as anthroposophy.

If we look at what was intended with the Theosophical Society in terms of—let me put it like this—the people as a group, we have to begin by looking into the consciousness of these people, looking into the souls of these people in order to understand the nature of the their consciousness. After all, these people gave expression to their consciousness in the way they went about things. They assembled, held meetings, lectures and discussions. They also met outside meetings, indeed talked a great deal with one another in smaller groups. It was not customary at general meetings, for instance, that the time was filled in the way as was the case with us yesterday. Opportunities were always found to have a meal together, or a cup of tea and so on. People even found time to change dress in the intervals. It was really what might be described as a reflection of the kind of social behaviour we might find in daily life. But that, of course, is something that is of less interest to us. Our interest must be in the consciousness of the people. And here it was particularly noticeable that there were highly contradictory forces at play between these personalities.

These contradictory forces were particularly noticeable when these people held meetings. They came together. But everyone who was not a dyed-in-the-wool theosophist sought to have two ideas about every person. The peculiar thing was that when you came to the Theosophical Society it was simply necessary to have two ideas about each person. The one idea was the one you formed as a result of the way they approached you. But the other was the idea which everyone else had of each individual. This was based on very generalized ideas about the nature of human beings, about universal human love, about being advanced—as they called it—or not, about the way you had to be in a serious mood in order to prove worthy of receiving the doctrines of theosophy, and so on. These were pretty theoretical considerations. And everyone thought that something of all this had to be present in the people walking around there in flesh and blood. The naive impressions of the other person I referred to first were not really alive in the members, but each one had an image of all the others which was based on theoretical ideas about human beings and human behaviour.

No one actually saw anyone else as they really were, but rather as a kind of spectre. And thus it was necessary on meeting Mr Miller, for example, and forming a naive impression of Mr Miller, to form a spectral idea of him when visualizing what someone else thought of Mr Miller. Because no one had the real idea of the other but a spectre presented itself which was a construct. Thus it was necessary to have two ideas about each person. However, most of the members dispensed with the idea of the real person and merely absorbed the idea of the spectre, so that in reality members always perceived one another in spectral form. The consciousness of the members was filled with spectres. You simply had to have an interest in psychology.

A certain generosity and lack of preconceptions was also required to take a real interest. It was, after all, very interesting to be involved in what existed there as a kind of spectral society. Because in the boundary I just spoke about it was a spectral society which lived there. That was particularly evident with regard to the leading personalities. The leading personalities lived in the perception of the others in a very peculiar manner. Reference might be made to a leading personality—let us call them X. During the night their astral form went from house to house—only members' houses, of course—as an invisible helper. All kinds of things emanated from them. The spectral ideas about leading personalities were in part extraordinarily beautiful. Often, it was a considerable contrast to meet these leading personalities in the flesh. But the general mood then ensured that as far as possible only the spectral idea was allowed to exist and the real idea was not permitted to intrude.

A certain view of things, a doctrine, was definitely required for this. Since not everyone is clairvoyant, although there were many people at the time who at least pretended to be—we won't examine right now the extent to which this was true—but since not everyone was clairvoyant, certain theories were necessary to concoct the spectres which were formed there.

Now these theories had something exceedingly archaic about them. It was hard to avoid the impression that these spectral human constructs were assembled according to old, rehashed theories. In many cases it was easy to find the ancient writings which provided the source material.

Thus on top of their spectral nature these human spectres were not of the present time. They were actually people from earlier incarnations; people who gave the impression of having clambered out of Egyptian, Persian or ancient Indian graves. In a certain sense any feeling of the present had been lost.

But there was additionally something else entirely. These ancient doctrines were difficult to understand, even when clothed in relatively modern terminology. Now there was much talk about these ancient doctrines in abstract forms. The physical body was still called the physical body. The etheric body was borrowed from medieval concepts, as was perhaps the astral body. But then there were the things like manas, kama manas and suchlike, which everybody talked about but no one really understood what they were. How could they, when all of it was clothed in very modern, materialistic ideas? These teachings contained cosmic contexts, cosmic concepts and ideas so that you could get a feeling that souls were talking here in a language not of centuries, but of millennia past.

This went very far. Books were written in such an idiom. They were translated; and it all happened in such forms. But there was another side to all this. It had its beautiful aspect, because despite the superficial use of words, despite the lack of understanding, something did rub off on people. We might almost say that, even if it did not enter their souls, an extraordinary amount adhered to the outer garment of their souls. They went about not exactly with an awareness of the etheric body or kama manas, but they had an awareness that they were enveloped in layers of coats: one of them the etheric body, another kama manas and so on. They were proud of these coats, of this dress of the soul, and that provided a strong element of cohesion among them.

This was something which forged the Theosophical Society into a single entity in an exceptionally intense manner, which created a tremendous communal spirit in which every single person felt themselves to be a representative of the Theosophical Society. This Society was something in itself; beyond each individual member, the Society itself had what might be described as an awareness of itself. It had its own I. This own I was so strong that even when the absurdities of its leaders eventually came to light in a rather bizarre manner, those people, once they felt they belonged, held tight with an iron grip and thus had the feeling: it is akin to treachery if people do not stick together, even if the Society's leaders have committed grave mistakes.

Anyone who has gained an insight into the struggles which certain members of the Theosophical Society later went through long after the Anthroposophical Society had separated itself, when people repeatedly realized the terrible things their leaders were doing but failed to see that as a sufficient reason to leave—anyone who saw the struggles that went on in the individual souls will, even if there has to be condemnation of really terrible things, have on the other hand developed a certain respect for this consciousness of its self of the Society as a whole.

And that leads us to ask whether the conditions which surrounded the birth of the Anthroposophical Society might not allow a similar consciousness of the Society to develop?

From its foundation, the Anthroposophical Society had to manage without the often very questionable means by which the Theosophical Society established its strong cohesion and consciousness of its self.[16] The Anthroposophical Society had to be guided by the ideal: wisdom can only be found in truth.[17] But this is something which has remained an ideal until now. In this area in particular, the Anthroposophical Society leaves a lot to be desired, having barely begun to address the development of a communal body, an identity of its own.

The Anthroposophical Society is a collection of people who strive very hard as individual human beings. But as a society it hardly exists, precisely because this feeling of a common bond is not there, as only the smallest number of members of the Anthroposophical Society feel themselves to be representatives of the Society. Everyone feels that they are an individual and forgets altogether that there is supposed to be an Anthroposophical Society.

Having now characterized the people—I will still add to this in the following days—I would still like to characterize the other side. Because how has anthroposophy positioned itself in all these strivings, as I have to call them, of our time? Anyone who wants to, can find the principles of anthroposophy in my *Philosophy of Freedom*.[18] I wish to highlight just one thing today, which is that this *Philosophy of Freedom* refers with inner necessity to a spiritual realm which is, for example, the source of our moral impulses. So that, as set out in *The*

*Philosophy of Freedom*, we cannot stop at the sensory world but have to progress to a spiritual realm founded in itself. After all, the existence of a spiritual realm still acquires the quite different concrete form that the human being in their innermost being, when they become aware of their innermost being, is not connected to the sensory world but to the spiritual world.

These are the two basic points made in *The Philosophy of Freedom*: first, that there is a spiritual realm and, second, that a person is connected with the innermost I of their being to this spiritual realm. Inevitably the question arose as to whether it is possible to make public in this way what was to be revealed to contemporary humankind as a kind of message about the spiritual world. Is there a way to connect to anything? After all, you cannot simply stand up and talk into thin air. Mind you, all kinds of odd proposals have kept coming recently. When I was in Vienna in 1918, for instance, I was summoned, by telegram no less, to go to the Rax Alp on the northern boundary of Styria, stand up on that mountain and there deliver a lecture for the Alps! I need hardly add that I did not respond to it. But you cannot speak to mountains or into thin air. You must create a link with something which already exists in contemporary culture. And basically there were few opportunities like that around at the turn of the nineteenth to the twentieth century. There were people whose striving at the time was to join the Theosophical Society. Ultimately these were the ones to whom it was possible to talk about these things.

But a feeling of responsibility towards the people whom we were addressing was not enough; a feeling of responsibility towards the spiritual world was also required, and in particular towards the form in which it appeared at that time. And here I might draw attention to the way in which what was to become anthroposophy gradually emerged from those endeavours which I did not yet publicly call anthroposophy. I just want to present the facts today and then thread the connections before you in the next few days.

In the 1880s I could see, above all, a kind of mirage; something which looked quite natural in the physical world but which, nevertheless, took on a deeper significance in a certain sense, even when taken as an insubstantial mirage, a play of the light. If you opened yourself in a contemporary way to the way the worldview developed which lived in the culture of the time—few people engaged with it but they nevertheless existed—you were liable to encounter something very peculiar. If we think just about Central Europe in the first instance, there was what I might describe as the world-shattering philosophy which wanted to be everything, which wanted to be a whole world-view: the philosophy of idealism from the first half of the nineteenth century. There were echoes of, let us say, Fichte's, Hegel's and Solger's[19] philosophies which at the time they were developed meant as much to some of their adherents as anthroposophy can ever mean to people today. But they were basically a sum of abstract concepts.

Take a look at the first of the three parts of Hegel's *Encyclopedia of Philosophy*[20] and you will find a series of concepts which are developed one from the other. It starts with being. Then comes nothingness. Then comes becoming. Then comes existence. I cannot, of course, describe the whole of Hegelian logic now because it is a thick book, and it continues like this with such concepts. Lastly there is purpose. There are only abstract thoughts and ideas.

And yet this is what Hegel called it: God before the creation of the world. So that we have to imagine that if we raised the question: What was God like before the creation of the world? we would get a system of abstract concepts and abstract ideas.

Now when I was young—that is a long time ago—there lived in Vienna a Herbartian philosopher called Robert Zimmermann.[21] He said that today—he meant 'today' as in the last third of the nineteenth century—we should no longer be permitted to think in the Hegelian mode, or that of Solger or similar philosophers. Because how did those people think?

You see, according to Zimmermann these people thought as if they themselves were God. Zimmermann actually had a very peculiar way of thinking for a philosopher, but a very characteristic one. He said, Hegel thought as if he himself were God. That was almost as if someone from the then Theosophical Society had spoken, for there was a member, indeed a leading member of the Theosophical Society, Franz Hartmann,[22] who said in all his lectures something to the effect that you had to become aware of the God within yourself, each person had something like a divine human being, a God within themselves, and when that God began to speak you were speaking theosophy. Franz Hartmann, when he let his divine human being speak, indeed said all kinds of things that I don't want to judge now. But Hegel, when in Zimmermann's view he allowed the God within himself to speak, said: Being, nothingness, becoming, existence; and then the world was first of all logically put in a state of turbulence, whereupon it flipped over into its otherness, and then nature was there.

Robert Zimmermann, however, said: That must no longer be allowed, for that is theosophy. We should no longer have any theosophy today, Robert Zimmermann said in the eighties; we can no longer accept the theosophy of Schelling, of Solger, of Hegel. We must not allow the God in human beings to speak, for that leads to a theocentric perspective. That is only something we can strive for if we behave rather like Icarus: you know, you slip up in the cosmos and take a fall! You have to remain grounded in the human perspective. And so Robert Zimmermann wrote his *Anthroposophy* to counter the theosophy of Hegel, Schelling, Solger and others, whom he also treats as theosophists in his *History of Aesthetics*. It is from this *Anthroposophy*[23] that I later took the name. I found the book exceedingly interesting then as a phenomenon of the time. The only thing is that this *Anthroposophy* is an assembly of the most horribly abstract concepts. It consists of three parts. Then it has subsidiary chapters: firstly the logical ideas, secondly the aesthetic ideas, thirdly the ethical ideas.

You see—if in the first instance we disregard aesthetics that deals with art, and ethical ideas that deal with human behaviour—human beings are, after all, looking for something in the worldview that is offered them which will satisfy their inner selves, which will give them the ability to say that they are connected with a divine-spiritual realm, that they possess something eternal. Zimmermann was seeking an answer to the question: When human beings go beyond mere sensory existence, when they become truly aware of their spiritual human nature, what can they know? They know logical ideas.

Hegel, after all, at least wrote a whole book of such logical ideas. Yet those are ideas which only a God can think. But if it is not a God in human beings who is thinking, but human beings themselves, then five logical ideas emerge, at least with Robert Zimmermann. First, the necessity of thinking; second, the equivalence of concepts; third, the combination of concepts; fourth, the differentiation of concepts; and fifth, the law of contradiction: something can only be itself or something else, no third option is available. That, my dear friends, is the extent of what is being stated here, summarized in abstract ideas; that is, those things which the human being can know when they detach themselves from the world of the senses, when they relate to what is soul and spirit in them.

If this *Anthroposophy* were the only thing available to people, we would have to say that everything that people once had in the various religious faiths, in religious ritual and so on, must be seen as a thing of the past; what is seen as Christianity must be seen as a thing of the past because these things in turn can only be derived from history and so on. When a person thinks only of what they can know as anthropos, what they can know when they make their soul independent of sensory impressions, of worldly history, it is this: I know that I must submit to the necessity of thinking, to the equivalence of concepts, the combination of concepts, differentiation, and the law of contradiction. That, whatever name it is given, was all there was.

This was then supplemented by aesthetic ideas. These are the ideas of perfection, concord, harmony; once again it is five ideas. And equally there are five ethical ideas. The aesthetic ideas still include antagonism and the concord of antagonism.

First the logical ideas: the necessity of thinking, equivalence, combination, differentiation, law of contradiction.

Second the aesthetic ideas: perfection, concord, harmony, antagonism, concord of antagonism.

Third the ethical ideas: and in the five ethical ideas—ethical perfection, benevolence, justice, conflict, resolution of conflict—lives the basis for human action.

As you can see, that has all been put in an exceedingly abstract form. And it is preceded by the title: *Anthroposophy—An Outline*.

You can see that a great deal was meant by this from the dedication that preceded it. In this dedication there are, I would say, touching lines. It says—I can't quote verbatim, but roughly—'To Harriet. It was you who prompted me, when night began to darken around my eyes, to combine the scattered ideas that had long lived in me into this book. And a willing hand was found to write down what I had conceived in the dark chamber.'

So it is pointed out in a very beautiful language that the author had an eye disease, had to spend some time in a dark chamber where he thought up these ideas, and that then a willing hand found itself to write them down. These dedicatory lines then conclude very beautifully by saying: And so no one can deny that this book, like the light itself, emerged from the darkness.

You can see that it was like a mirage: very peculiar. Robert Zimmermann produced an *Anthroposophy* in this sense out of theosophy. But I do not believe that if I had lectured on his kind of *Anthroposophy* we would ever have had an anthroposophical movement. The name, however, was very well chosen. And I took on the name when, for fundamental reasons which will become clear in the course of these lectures, I had to start dealing with various things, starting with the spiritual fact—a certainty for everyone with access to the spiritual world—of repeated lives on earth.

But if we do not deal with such things frivolously but with a feeling of spiritual responsibility, they have to be put in a context. I have to say that it became extraordinarily difficult at the turn of the nineteenth to the twentieth century to put repeated lives on earth into a context which would have been understood at that time. But there were points where such a link could be established. And before going any further I want to tell you how I myself sought to make use of such points of contact.

There is a very interesting synopsis of anthropological truths by Topinard.[24] The concluding chapter—it was a book which was often cited at the time, less so today, today it is already somewhat outdated in its details, but it is cleverly written—contains a nice synopsis. And there, in a way that everyone who was of a modern consciousness at the time subscribed to, could be found in Topinard a collation of all the biological facts that led to the thought of the animal species as arising from each other, one from the other. Topinard was indeed able to invoke everything that had been discussed in his book. So everything could be found that led people to believe that a transformation takes place from animal species to animal species. Topinard stays with the facts and says, after he has mentioned about twenty-two points I think, that the twenty-third is then what he cites as this transformation of the animal species. But now we are faced with the problem of the human being. He leaves that unanswered. What happens there?

Now, by taking the biological theory of evolution very seriously, it was possible to build on such an author and say, this is where he leaves the question open. If we continue, and add point twenty-three to point twenty-two, we reach the conclusion that the animal species keep repeating themselves at a higher level. In the human being we progress to the individual. Once the individual has repeated themselves, we have reincarnation. As you can see, I tried to make use of what was available to me, and in that form attempted to make something comprehensible to the whole world which is, in any case, present before the soul as a spiritual fact. But in order to provide a point of access for people in general, something had to be used which was already in existence but which did not come to an end with a full stop, but with a dash. I simply continued beyond the dash where natural science left off. That was the first thing. I delivered that lecture[25] to the group which I mentioned yesterday. It was not well received because no one was interested in science. It was not felt necessary to reflect on the issues raised by the sciences, and of course it seemed superfluous to those people that the things in which they believed should additionally need to be supported by evidence.

The second thing was that at the beginning of the century I delivered a lecture cycle entitled 'From Buddha to Christ' to a group which called itself Die Kommenden.[26] In these lectures I tried to depict the line of development from Buddha to Christ and to present Christ as the culmination of what had existed previously. The lecture cycle concluded with the interpretation of the Gospel of John which starts with the raising of Lazarus. Thus the Lazarus issue, as represented in my *Christianity As Mystical Fact*,[27] forms the conclusion of the lecture cycle 'From Buddha to Christ'.

This coincided roughly with the time when I was then approached by the group which had invited me to give the lectures which are collected in my book *Mystics after Modernism* with regard to the task of addressing theosophists on matters which I both needed and wanted to speak about. That occurred at the same time as the endeavour to establish a German Section of the Theosophical Society.[28] And before I had even become a member, or indeed shown the slightest inclination to become a member, I was called upon to become the General Secretary of this German Section of the Theosophical Society.

When the German Section was being founded, I delivered a cycle of lectures which were attended by, I think, only two or three theosophists, and otherwise by members of the group to which I had addressed the lectures 'From Buddha to Christ'.[29] This group was called 'Die Kommenden'. The names tended to stay with me. It must be connected with some law. Robert Zimmermann's *Anthroposophy* remained, 'Die Kommenden' occurred again in the name of 'Der Kommende Tag'.[30] Such names stay with you, old names.

For this group—to which, as I said, at most two or three theosophists had gone, and these really only out of curiosity—I spoke about the development of worldviews from the oldest oriental times to the present, or anthroposophy. This cycle of lectures was to begin with given the full title: 'The history of the development of humanity with reference to the worldviews from oldest oriental times to the present day, or anthroposophy'. This lecture cycle—I have to keep mentioning this—was given by me at the same time as the German Section of the Theosophical Society was being established. I even left the meeting, and while everyone else was continuing their discussions and talking about theosophy, I was delivering my lecture cycle on anthroposophy.

One of those who then turned from theosophist into good anthroposophist, indeed someone who became a very good anthroposophist, went at the time to this anthroposophical lecture cycle and said to me afterwards that what I had said did not accord at all with what Mrs Besant was saying and what Blavatsky was saying. I replied, then that is how it is no doubt. In other words, someone with a good knowledge of all the dogmas of theosophy had discovered correctly that something was wrong. Even at that time it was possible to say that it was simply wrong, that something else applied.

So these are the facts I put before you to begin with. I now want to put to you another apparently completely unconnected fact which I referred to yesterday.

There were Blavatsky's books, the main ones to begin with: *Isis Unveiled* and *The Secret Doctrine*. There really was no reason to be terribly enthusiastic about the kind of people who took what was written in these books as holy dogma. But for the reasons advanced yesterday it was possible to see these books as something exceedingly interesting, and above all it was possible to see Blavatsky herself as an exceedingly interesting phenomenon, if only from a deeper psychological point of view. Why? Well, you see, there is a tremendous difference between the two books *Isis Unveiled* and Blavatsky's *Secret Doctrine;* there is a tremendous difference. This difference will become most clearly apparent to you if I tell you how those familiar with similar things judged these two books. What do I mean when I refer to those familiar with such things?

Traditions have been preserved, my dear friends, which have their origins in the most ancient mysteries and which were then kept by a number of so-called secret societies. Certain secret societies also bestowed degrees on their members, who advanced from the first degree to the second and the third and so on. As they did so, they were told certain things on the basis of those traditions. At the lower degrees people did not understand this knowledge but accepted it as holy dogma. In fact they did not understand it at the higher degrees either. But even if neither the lower degrees nor higher ones understood these traditions, there was the firm belief among the members of the lower degrees that the members of the higher degrees understood everything. This belief existed very firmly.

Nevertheless, a pure form of knowledge had been preserved. A great deal was known if we simply take the texts. You need do no more—today, where everything is printed and everything is becoming accessible, these things can easily be accessed—than pick up these things which have been printed, and revitalize them with what you know from anthroposophy—for you cannot revitalize it in any other way—and you will see that these traditions contain great, ancient and majestic knowledge even in the distorted form in which it is often printed today. Sometimes the words sound completely wrong, but everyone who has any insight is aware that they have their origin in ancient wisdom. But the real distinguishing mark of the activity in these secret societies was that people had a general feeling that there were human beings in earlier times who were initiates, and who were able to speak about the world, the cosmos and the spiritual realm on the basis of an ancient wisdom. And they knew how to construct sentences; they had something to say about what was handed down. There were many such people.

Then Blavatsky's *Isis Unveiled* appeared. The people who were particularly shocked by its publication were those who held traditional knowledge through their attainment of lower or higher degrees in the secret societies. They usually justified their reaction by saying that the time was not yet ripe to make available through publication to humanity in general the things which were being kept hidden in the secret societies. That was what people thought. It was even their honest opinion that the time was simply not ripe to tell humanity in general about them in print. But there were a number of people who had another reason. And this reason can really be understood only if I draw your attention to another set of facts.

In the fifth post-Atlantean period, specifically in the nineteenth century, everything actually passed over into abstract concepts and ideas, so that at last one of the deepest, most important intellects framed his worldview in the abstract concepts of being, nothingness, becoming, existence, and finally purpose. Everything in this earlier modern era passed over into abstract concepts and ideas.

In Central Europe one of those who began with such abstract ideas was the philosopher Schelling.[31] At a time when these ideas could still enthuse others because they contained inner human emotional force, when Schlegel was listening to Tieck in Jena, when such abstract ideas were discussed with incredible enthusiasm, at that time Schelling was among those who taught such abstract ideas. A few years later Schelling no longer found any satisfaction in these abstract ideas and began to immerse himself in mysticism, specifically in Jakob Boehme,[32] allowing himself to be influenced by Boehme's thinking and extracting from it something which immediately took on a more real quality. But no one really understood it any longer, for no one could make sense of what Schelling wrote in *Philosophical Investigations into the Essence of Human Freedom*, 1809. In the 1820s, following a lengthy reclusive period, Schelling began to speak in a curious manner. In Reclam's Universalbibliothek you can find a small booklet by him called *Die Weltalter*. When you pick up this small volume you will get a strange feeling. You will say to yourself, all of this is still rather nebulous and abstract. But a curious feeling remains: why is it that this person, Schelling, doesn't actually say what was later then said on an anthroposophical basis for example as the truths about Atlantis but nearly—almost clumsily—hints at them? It is quite interesting, this small volume by Schelling in Reclam's Universalbibliothek, *Die Weltalter*.

But then Frederick William IV appointed him to the university in Berlin in 1841. There, Hegel having been dead for ten years, he became Hegel's successor. That is when Schelling began to lecture on his *Philosophy of Revelation*.

Even that is still terribly abstract. He talks about three 'powers A', 1, 2, 3. It is terribly abstract. But he then continues with this until he achieves some kind of grasp of the old mysteries, until he achieves some kind of grasp of Christianity. And once again we can get the feeling in the way he deals with these ideas: a path is being sought here, still in a very primitive way, into a real spiritual world. But it is difficult to really understand properly what Schelling briefly puts forward here. People didn't understand anything despite everything. It is, after all, not very easy to understand it because this was a dubious path.

All the same, there was something in the general awareness of the time—this is, after all, evidence of it—which led someone like Schelling to note that a spiritual world needed to be investigated.

This took a different form in England. It is exceedingly interesting to read the writings of Lawrence Oliphant.[33] Of course Oliphant presents his conclusions about the primeval periods of human development on earth in quite a different way, because the English approach is quite distinct from the German one; it is much more physical, down-to-earth, material. The two approaches are in a certain sense, taking into account differing national characteristics, parallel phenomena: Schelling in the early part of the nineteenth century with his idealism, Oliphant with his realism, both of them displaying a strong drive towards the spiritual world, a strong drive to understand the world which is revealed by the spirit to human beings.

If we investigate the remarkable thing here, both in Schelling and Oliphant—it is actually the same phenomenon we have here, only with different national characteristics—it is this: these two men grew into the culture of their time, one in a German, the other in an English way; they struggled on until they had taken the philosophical ideas of their time about human beings, the cosmos and so on to their ultimate conclusion.

Both Schelling in his way and Oliphant in his struggled on. Now, you know from my anthroposophical accounts that human beings develop in early life in a way which makes physical development concomitant with soul development. That ceases later on. As I told you, the Greeks continued to develop into their thirties in a way which involved real parallel development of the physical and spiritual. With Schelling and Oliphant something different happened from the average person of today. With them it was like this: they developed at first as normal people; for if you are a philosopher today you can of course be a perfectly normal person, perhaps even a subnormal person, but that only in passing. A person may develop a concept further, but then they come to a halt, if they are a normal person. Schelling and Oliphant did not come to a halt but as they grew older their souls suddenly became filled with the vitality of previous lives on earth; they began to remember ancient things from earlier incarnations: distant memories, unclear memories, arose in a natural way. Suddenly that struck people like a flash. Both Oliphant and Schelling were now suddenly seen in a different light.

Both struggle through, become normal philosophers, each in their own country. Then in their later years they begin to recall knowledge which they have known in earlier lives on earth, only now it is like a misty memory. At this point they begin to speak about the spiritual world. Even if these are unclear memories it is, nevertheless, something to be feared by those who have only been through the old style, traditional development, that they might spread and gain the upper hand. These people lived in terrible fear that human beings could be born with the facility to remember what they had experienced in the past and speak about it. Indeed, they thought: What will then happen to our principle of secrecy? Here we are, they thought, making members of the first, second, third grades and so on swear holy oaths, but what remains of our secrecy if human beings are now being born who can recall personally what we have preserved and kept under lock and key?

Then *Isis Unveiled* appeared! The notable thing about it was that it brought openly on to the book market a whole lot of things which were being kept hidden in secret societies. These people now faced a great problem: how had Blavatsky obtained the knowledge which they had kept locked away and for which people had sworn holy oaths? It was those who were particularly shocked by this who paid a great deal of attention to *Isis Unveiled*. So what had appeared with Blavatsky's book represented a real problem for those people who consciously experienced the spiritual life of the end of the nineteenth century.

Then *The Secret Doctrine* appeared. That only made things worse. As I said, I'm only presenting facts today. *The Secret Doctrine* presented a whole category of knowledge which was the preserve of the highest grades in the secret societies. Those who were shocked by the first book, and even more so by the second one, used all kinds of expressions to describe them both, because Blavatsky as a phenomenon had a terribly unsettling effect, particularly on the so-called initiates. *Isis Unveiled* was less frightening because Blavatsky was a chaotic personality who continuously interspersed material which contained deep wisdom with all kinds of stuff and nonsense. So the frightened, so-called initiates could at least still say about *Isis Unveiled* that in it what was true was not new and what was new was not true! That was the initial judgement about the book. People knew: the unpleasant fact for them was that things had been revealed. After all, the book was called *Isis Unveiled*. They reassured themselves by saying that someone somewhere must have done something that actually infringed their rights.

But when *The Secret Doctrine* appeared, containing a whole lot of material which even the highest grades did not know, they could no longer say: What is true is not new and what is new is not true. For it contained a whole lot of things which had not been preserved by tradition.

Thus in a rather strange and, indeed, confusing way, this woman represented what had been feared since Schelling and Lawrence Oliphant.

That is why I said that her personality is psychologically even more interesting than her books. Blavatsky was an important and notable phenomenon of the spiritual life of the late nineteenth century.

This is the extent to which I wanted to present the facts.

# LECTURE THREE

## DORNACH, 12 JUNE 1923

In wishing to describe the development of groupings which have a certain connection with the Anthroposophical Society, albeit much misunderstood today, I yesterday had to make reference to the impact of HP Blavatsky. I already tried to indicate the position of this personality in the intellectual life at the end of the nineteenth century. I had to make reference to this personality for the reason that at the end of the nineteenth century Blavatsky's works prompted those whom I described the day before yesterday as homeless souls to come together.

Even if Blavatsky's works have very little to do with what appeared as anthroposophy, I do not want simply to describe the history of the anthroposophical movement in these lectures but also to characterize those of its aspects which relate to the Society. And that requires the kind of background which I have given you in these two days.

Now it is of course very easy—if we want to be critical about the kind of spiritual striving as appeared in, let us say, the Theosophical Society—to dismiss everything that can be said about Blavatsky; it is very easy to castigate a phenomenon like Blavatsky by pointing to the questionable nature of some of the things we encounter in the biography of this personality.

I could give you any number of examples. I could tell you how, within the society which took its cue from Blavatsky's spiritual life, the view gained ground that certain insights about the spiritual world became known because physical letters, physical announcements, that is things written on paper, came from a source which did not lie within the physical world. Such documents were called the Mahatma Letters.[34] They were exhibited, were said not to have been written in the normal way or at least hadn't reached the place where they were produced in a normal way. It then became a rather sensational affair when in that house where, guided by HP Blavatsky, such letters had been produced all kinds of deceptively constructed sliding doors could be shown to exist, where these letters could be pushed in through such doors in the normal physical way, but by deception, into the room where they were then found as magic letters, and the like.

It is, of course, extremely easy for contemporaries to point these things out and then find it proven that such a personality as Blavatsky can simply be dismissed by saying that she was a fraud. Well, we shall have more to say about this side of the phenomena which took place around Blavatsky. But let us for the moment take another view, namely the view to ignore in the first instance everything which took place outwardly.

Certainly, there are objections. But let us ignore these objections for a moment. Let us not bother with all the things that happened externally and simply look at the works. Then you will come to the conclusion I described to you these days, the conclusion that Blavatsky's works consist to a large degree of dilettantish, muddled stuff, but that despite this they contain material which, if it is examined in the right way, can be understood as reproducing far-reaching insights into the spiritual world or from the spiritual world—however they were acquired. That simply cannot be denied, in spite of all the objections which are raised.

This, I believe, leads to an issue of extraordinary importance and significance in the spiritual history of civilization. Why is it that at the end of the nineteenth century revelations from the spiritual world became accessible, let us say from a problematic source, which merit detailed attention, even from the objective standpoint of spiritual science, if only as the basis for further investigation; revelations which say more about the fundamental laws of the world, the fundamental forces of the world than anything which has been discovered about its secrets through modern philosophy or other currents of thought? That does seem a significant question.

It contrasts with another phenomenon of cultural history which must not be forgotten when we speak about the conditions under which something like the Anthroposophical Society exists, connected in general with the striving to find ways into the spiritual world. This phenomenon of cultural history is namely that people's ability to discriminate, their surety of judgement, has suffered greatly and regressed in our time.

It is easy to be deceived about this by the enormous progress which has been made. But it is precisely when we look at the enormous progress which has been made in the context of the progression of intellectual life, to the extent that individual human personalities as discerning individuals participate in the progression of intellectual life, that we get some idea of the capacity which our age possesses to deal with phenomena which require the application of judgement.

Many examples could be quoted. I just want to take a few. Let me ask those, for example, who concern themselves with, say, electrical engineering, about the significance of Ohm's law. The answer will be, of course, that Ohm's law constitutes one of the foundations for the development of the whole field of electrical engineering. When Ohm[35] completed the initial work which was to prove fundamental for the later formulation of Ohm's law, his work was rejected as useless by an important university's philosophical faculty. If this faculty had had its way, there would be no electrical engineering today.

Take something else that is perhaps even more tangible for you: you all know the important role which the telephone today plays in the whole life of our culture. When Reis,[36] who was not part of the official scientific establishment, initially wrote down the idea of the telephone and submitted his manuscript to one of the most famous journals of the time, the *Poggendorffsche Annalen*, his work was rejected as unusable. That is the power of judgement which people have and such examples could be infinitely multiplied! That indeed is the power of judgement of our time. One simply has to face up to these things in a fully objective manner.

You need only pick a subject at, let me say, the pinnacle of our culture—you will find similar things everywhere. Or if we go more into the hidden nooks and crannies, there are occasional fine examples which characterize the power of judgement among those who set the tone in administering, say, our cultural life. And the public, the general public moving along the broad highway—I spoke about it the day before yesterday—is in turn completely spellbound by what is deemed acceptable by these standards today. Well, this culture is prevalent in all countries; no country is better or worse than any other.

Take one such phenomenon: Adalbert Stifter[37] is a very significant writer, but I don't want to deal here with his importance as a writer but tell you something about his life. He went through his academic studies in school, indeed with excellent results, then studied science and wanted to become a teacher in a school with an academic orientation. Unfortunately he was thought to be totally unsuited to become a teacher in such a school, he was thought not talented enough to become a teacher in such a school. Coincidentally a certain Baroness Mink, who had nothing to do with judging the ability of teachers in schools with an academic orientation, heard about Adalbert Stifter as a writer, acquainted herself with the material he had produced so far—which he himself did not think was particularly good—and prevailed upon him to have it published. That caused a great stir. The authorities suddenly took the view that there was no one better equipped to become the schools' inspector for the whole country. And thus a person who a short while before had been thought not talented enough to become a teacher was suddenly appointed to supervise the work of every other teacher!

It would be an exceedingly interesting exercise to examine these things in all areas of our intellectual life, starting with phenomena such as I have just described with Adalbert Stifter and extending to, well, for example also a phenomenon like Julius Robert Mayer.[38] As you know, I have called into question the application under certain circumstances of the law of conservation of energy, which attaches to his name. But contemporary physics doesn't call it into question and defends this law unconditionally as one of its pillars.

Julius Robert Mayer, who today is regarded a hero—I have already mentioned others, such as Gregor Mendel, who suffered a similar fate—Julius Robert Mayer, who was born in Heilbronn on the Neckar, was always bottom of his class and was advised one day by the university he then attended—it was in Tübingen—to leave the university because of his performance. The university can certainly take no credit for the discoveries he made, because it wanted to send him down before he sat the exams which enabled him to become a doctor.

It would be interesting to describe these things in context, starting from such things up to and including the immense tragedy attached to the name of Semmelweis,[39] the personality to whose immense credit it is that puerperal fever has been reduced to a minimum today which before Semmelweis appeared was just killing people—up to and including the immense tragedy of Semmelweis which ultimately led, as with Julius Robert Mayer, to Semmelweis ending up in an insane asylum despite the fact that he is one of the greatest benefactors of humanity.

If all this material were seen in context, it would reveal an exceedingly important element in contemporary cultural history; an element through which it would be possible to demonstrate the weakness of this age of materialistic progress in recognizing the significance of spiritual events; how little there was an inclination to engage with what was coming over the horizon of intellectual life.

Such things have to be taken into account when taking full stock of the hostile forces opposing the intervention of spiritual movements. It is necessary to be aware of the general level of judgement which is applied in our time, an age which is excessively arrogant, precisely about its non-existent capacity to reach the right conclusions.

It was, after all, a very characteristic event that many of the things traditionally preserved by secret societies, which were at pains to prevent them reaching the public, should suddenly be published by a woman, Blavatsky, in a book called *Isis Unveiled*. Of course people were shocked when they realized that this book contained a great deal of the material which they had always kept under lock and key. And these societies, I might add, were considerably more concerned about their locks and keys than is our present Anthroposophical Society.

It was certainly not the intention of the Anthroposophical Society to secrete away everything contained in the lecture cycles. At a certain point I was requested to make the material, which I otherwise discuss verbally, accessible to a larger circle. And since there was no time to revise the lectures they were printed as manuscripts in a form in which they would otherwise not have been published—not because I did not want to publish the material, but because I did not want to publish it in this form and, furthermore, because there was concern that it should be read by people who have the necessary preparation in order to prevent misunderstanding. Even so, it is now possible to acquire every lecture cycle, even for the purpose of attacking us.

The societies which kept specific knowledge under lock and key and made people swear oaths that they would not reveal any of it, made a better job of protecting these things. They knew that something special must have occurred when a book suddenly appeared which revealed something of significance in the sense that we have discussed. As for the insignificant material—well, you need only go to one of the side-streets in Paris and you can buy the writings of the secret societies by the lorry load. But the publication of those writings will not be of any great concern for those who preserved the traditional knowledge in the secret societies for as a rule these publications are worthless.

But *Isis Unveiled* was not worthless. *Isis Unveiled* was substantive enough to identify the knowledge which it presented as something original, through which was revealed the ancient wisdom which had been carefully guarded until that moment.

As I said, those who reacted with shock imagined that something specific was behind it, that someone had betrayed them. I do not want to focus so much on the internals of the matter in these lectures, what facts lie behind the scenes; I have discussed this repeatedly from a variety of angles in previous lectures.[40] But I now want rather to touch on the externals, to characterize the judgement of the world, because that is particularly relevant to the history of the movement. After all, it was not difficult to understand that someone who was initiated into these things, who had inherited traditional knowledge might have suggested it to Blavatsky for whatever reason, and it need not have been a particularly laudable one. People could say that very easily. It would not be far from the truth to state that the betrayal occurred in one or a number of secret societies and that Blavatsky was chosen to publish the material. But there would also have been other ways of getting such things out to the public than to make use of a lady, such as Blavatsky was, for this publication.

There was, however, a good reason to make use of this lady in particular, something I also want to characterize only from its external side. And here we come to a chapter in tracing our intellectual history which is really rather peculiar. At the time when Blavatsky appeared with her books, there was very, very little talk of a subject which today is on everyone's lips: psychoanalysis. But the appearance of Blavatsky in particular enabled the people of sound judgement who came into contact with this peculiar development to experience something in a living way which made what has been written so far by the various leading authorities in the psychoanalytic field appear amateurish in the extreme—as I put it recently in a different context. For what is it that psychoanalysis wishes to demonstrate?

Where psychoanalysis is correct in a certain sense is in its demonstration that there is something in the depths of human nature which, in whatever form it exists there, can be raised to consciousness and then goes beyond what human beings have in their consciousness to begin with. So that we can say, if you like, there is something present in the body which, when it is raised to consciousness, appears as something spiritual. There is something spiritual acting up in the body. It is, of course, an extremely primitive action for a psychiatrist to raise what remains of past experience from the depths of the human psyche in this way; past experience which has not been assimilated intensively enough to satisfy the emotional needs of a person, so that it sinks to the bottom, as it were, and settles there as a sediment, creating an unstable rather than a stable equilibrium. And that the things which have happened in the life of a person, although they act up down there in the unconscious, are then raised and when they are raised to consciousness turn out to be something spiritual which, we might say, just doesn't properly fit into the person's being; and therefore they act up improperly but once brought to consciousness can be come to terms with, thus liberating the person from their improper presence.

But now it is interesting to see what such amateurish psycho-analytical research has found today. In Jung,[41] in particular, that is very interesting. It occurred to him that somewhere down there—of course there is some difficulty in defining down there, it just is somewhere down there, an indeterminate being—there are all the experiences which a person has failed to come to terms with since birth; that down there in a person's being there are all kinds of things that refer back to the primal father, indeed refer back completely to all experiences of the races and further back. So today it no longer seems impossible to the psychiatrist that, for example, what was experienced, let's say as the Oedipus problem in Greece, made an impression on people. Then it was passed down and down and down. And today some poor soul goes to the psychiatrist who psychoanalyses them and discovers something so deep-seated in the psyche that it did not originate in their present life, but came through their father, grandfather, great-grandfather and so on, until we arrive at the ancient Greeks who experienced the Oedipus problem. So it was passed down through the blood and today can be psycho-analysed away. These Oedipal feelings act up in the person and can be psychoanalysed away. People then even believe that they have discovered some very interesting connections through their ability to psychoanalyse away what lies in the far distant past of the race.

Well, you see, these are quite amateurish research methods. You need only have a basic knowledge of anthroposophy to know that all kinds of things can be extracted from the depths of a person's being. First there is our life before birth, pre-earthly life, the things which the human being has experienced before they descended into the physical world, and then there are those things which they experienced in earlier lives on earth. That takes you from an amateurish approach to reality!

But we also learn to recognize how the human psyche contains in furled up form, as it were, the secrets of the cosmos. Indeed, that was the view of past ages, that the secrets of the cosmos unfurl when a person raises everything that is hidden within them. That is why the human being was described as a microcosm, not because of the frippery that is so often used today, but because the experience was actually there that all kinds of things can be raised from the depths of the human being which lie concealed in the vastness of the cosmos.

What we encounter as psychoanalysis today really is amateurish in the extreme. On the one hand it is psychologically amateurish because it does not recognize that at certain levels physical and spiritual life become one. It considers the superficial life of the soul in abstract terms, and does not advance to the level where this soul life weaves creatively in the blood and in the breathing—in other words, where it is united with our so-called material functions. The soul life is considered amateurishly. But, secondly, the physical life is also amateurishly conceived, because it is observed purely in its outer physical aspects and there is no understanding that the spiritual is present everywhere in physical life, and above all in the human organism. When two amateurish views are interwoven in such a way that the one is supposed to illuminate the other, as psychoanalysis does, then these amateurish approaches do not simply add up but are multiplied. We have amateurism squared.

Well, the manifestation of this kind of amateurism squared could certainly be seen in the psychological problem that is Blavatsky. A stimulus may have come from somewhere, through some betrayal. This stimulus had the same effect as if—in this case—a wise and invisible psychiatrist had triggered within her a great amount of knowledge which originated in her own personality rather than from ancient writings handed down by tradition. Something had emerged from that person's being itself through what I might call the invisible psychiatrist. For if there was a traitor, they weren't the psychiatrist; they only gave the stimulus. But it was the circumstances that gave the stimulus! What circumstances?

If you look at development up to the fifteenth century or thereabouts, you will find that it was not an infrequent occurrence for revelations of cosmic secrets to be triggered within human beings by something—it need have been nothing more than some particularly characteristic outer phenomenon. Later this became an extremely mystical event. The tale told about Jakob Boehme,[42] who had a magnificent vision as he looked at a pewter bowl, is admired because people do not know that in earlier times up into the fifteenth century it was very common for an apparently minor stimulus to provoke in human beings tremendous visions of cosmic secrets, which were then seen by the person.

But it has become increasingly rare that human beings have been able to have inner revelations in response to such stimuli. That is due to the increasing dominance of the intellect. Intellectualism is connected with a specific development of the brain. The brain— although this cannot, of course, be demonstrated externally in anatomy and physiology, it can nevertheless be shown spiritually— calcifies in a certain sense, becomes hardened. This hardened brain simply does not permit the inner vision of human beings to rise to the surface of consciousness.

And now I have to say something extremely paradoxical, which is nevertheless true. A greater hardening of the brain took place in men, ignoring exceptions which, of course, exist both in men and women—which is not to say that this is a particular reason for female brains to celebrate, for at the end of the nineteenth century they became hard enough too. But it was nevertheless men who were ahead in terms of a more pronounced intellectualism and hardening of the brain. And that is connected with their increasing inability to form judgements.

Now this was exactly the same time at which the secrecy surrounding the knowledge of ancient times was still very pronounced. It became obvious that this knowledge had little effect on men. They learnt it by rote as they rose through the degrees. They were not really affected by it and kept it under lock and key. But if someone wished to make this ancient wisdom flower once more, there was a special experiment he could try, and that was to make a small dose of this knowledge, which he need not even necessarily have understood himself, available to a woman whose brain might have been prepared in a special way—for Blavatsky's brain was something quite different from the brains of other nineteenth-century women. Thus material which was otherwise dried-up old knowledge was able to ignite, in a manner of speaking, in these female brains through the contrast with what was otherwise available as culture; was able to stimulate Blavatsky in the same way that the psychiatrist stimulates the whole human being through some instruction or other. By this means she was able to find within herself what had been forgotten altogether by that section of humanity which did not belong to the secret societies, and had been kept carefully under lock and key and not understood by those who did belong. In this way what I might describe as a cultural escape valve was created which allowed this knowledge to emerge.

But at the same time there was simply no basis on which it could have been dealt with in a sensible manner. For Mrs Blavatsky was certainly no logician. Logic was not in any way her strong suit. While she was able to reveal cosmic secrets because of her nature as a whole, she was not capable of presenting these things in a form which could be justified before the modern scientific conscience.

Now just ask yourselves how, given the paucity of judgement with which spiritual phenomena were received, was there any chance of correctly assessing their re-emergence only twenty years later in a very basic and dilettantish form in psychoanalysis, and only in a very small area? How was proper account to be taken of something which had the potential to become an overwhelming experience, but to which psychoanalysis can only aspire once it has been cleansed and clarified and stands on a firm basis, when it is practised with scientific rigour; when it is no longer founded on the blood which has flowed down from the people who experienced the Oedipus problem to our present generation, but encompasses a true understanding of cosmic relationships? How was such experience, which presents a magnificent uncaricatured counter-image to today's impaired psychoanalytical research, to be assimilated adequately within a wider context in an age in which the ability to form true judgements was such as I have described? In this respect there were some interesting experiences to be had with regard to the view that could be encountered in our time if you made even just an attempt to appeal to a slightly broader judgement.

Let me illustrate this with an example of how difficult it is in our modern age to make yourself understood if you want to appeal to broader, more generous powers of judgement; you will see from the remainder of the lectures how necessary it is that I deal with these apparently purely personal matters.

There was a period at the turn of the century in Berlin, where I lived at the time, during which a number of Giordano Bruno associations were being established, including a Giordano Bruno League. There were also other Giordano Bruno associations, but a Giordano Bruno League was set up. Its membership included some really excellent people in tune with the time who had a thorough interest in everything contemporary which merited the focus of a person's ideas, feelings and will. And in the abstract way in which these things happen in our age, the Giordano Bruno League even also referred to the spirit. A well-known figure[43] who belonged to this League titled his inaugural lecture 'No Matter without Spirit'. But all this lacked real perspective, because the spirit and the ideas which were being pursued there were fundamentally so abstract that they could not approach the reality of the world. The way of thinking was terribly abstract. What annoyed me particularly was that these people introduced the concept of monism at every available opportunity. Homage had to be paid to monism which was the only reasonable thing to do and appropriate for humanity, and dualism was such old hat. This was always followed with the remark that the modern age had escaped from the dualism of the Middle Ages.

These were things which I found exceptionally annoying at the time. I was annoyed by the waffle about monism and the amateurish rejection of dualism. I was annoyed by the vague, pantheistic reference to the spirit: spirit which is present, well, simply everywhere. The word became devoid of content. I found all that pretty annoying. Actually I clashed with the speaker immediately after that first lecture on 'No Matter without Spirit', which did not go down well at all. But then all that monistic carry-on became more and more annoying, interesting but annoying, so I decided to tackle these people in the hope that I could at least inject some life into their powers of judgement. And since a whole series of lectures had already been devoted to tirades against the obscurantism of the Middle Ages, to the terrible dualism of scholasticism, I decided—this was the time at which people currently say that I was supposed to have been a rabid disciple of Haeckel—to do something to shake up this judgement.

I gave a lecture on Thomas Aquinas[44] and said, summarizing in a few sentences what I spoke about in detail at the time, approximately the following: there was no justification with regard to the ideas of the intellectual life of the past to refer to the Middle Ages as obscurantist, specifically in respect of the dualism of Thomism and scholasticism. As monism was constantly being used as a catchword, I intended to show that Thomas Aquinas had been a thorough monist. Only it was wrong to interpret monism solely in its present materialistic sense; everyone had to be considered a monist who saw the underlying principle of the world as a whole, as the *monon*. So I said that Thomas Aquinas had certainly done that, because he had naturally seen the *monon* in the divine unity underlying creation. This was based, I said, on the purest monism. Only he had made the distinction in accordance with his time that the one half could be grasped through ordinary human sensory and intellectual knowledge and the other through the kind of knowledge which was called faith at the time. But what scholasticism still understood as faith was not understood by contemporary humanity at all. One had to be clear, I said, that Thomas Aquinas had intended on the one hand to investigate the world through sensory research and intellectual knowledge but, on the other hand, that he had wanted to supplement this intellectual knowledge with the truths of revelation. But he had done that precisely to gain access to the *monon* of the world. He had simply wanted to proceed using two approaches. The worst thing for the present age would be, I said, if it could not develop sufficiently broad concepts to embrace some sort of historical perspective.

In short, I wanted to inject some fluidity into their dried-out brains. But it was in vain because it had a quite extraordinary effect. To begin with, these people had not the slightest idea what to make of it. They were all Protestants and now they thought that Catholicism was to be introduced by the back door. They thought that Catholicism was to be defended with such terrible dualism. It is appalling, they said; we make every effort to deal Catholicism a mortal blow, and now a member of this self-same Giordano Bruno League comes along to defend it!

Truly, these people were wondering at the time whether I had not gone insane overnight when I gave that lecture. They could make nothing of it. And yet they were among the most enlightened people of their time. There was really only one who then appeared as a kind of apologist. That was the poet Wolfgang Kirchbach[45] who then thought up the formula under which the lecture in the Giordano Bruno League could be tolerated. This formula he thought up in the following way. He said, well, Steiner did not really intend to introduce Catholicism by the back door but he wanted to show that in that old scholastic wisdom of Catholicism there was something much more meaningful than what we ourselves have as our superficial concepts today. That is what he wanted to show us. He wanted to show us that Catholicism is such a strong enemy because we are such weak opponents, that we should acquire more powerful weapons. That is what he wanted to show with his lecture. This was the only formula which led to the lecture being tolerated by a third, by a minority, of the members so that at least I wasn't expelled from the Giordano Bruno League. But the majority thought I was a person who had been led to confusion by Catholicism.

Well, you see, that is one such episode from that time of which people now say that I was a rabid disciple of Haeckel. But it is through this kind of thing that we learn about powers of discrimination; specifically, the willingness to take a broadly based view of something which, above all, did not rely on theoretical formulations, but aimed to make real progress on the path to the spirit, to gain real access to the spiritual world.

Because whether or not we gain access to the spiritual world does not depend on whether we have this or that theory about spirit or matter, but whether we are in a position to achieve a real experience of the spiritual world. As I have often emphasized, spiritualists believe very firmly that all their actions are grounded in the spirit, but their theories are completely devoid of it. They most certainly do not lead human beings to the spirit. One can even be a materialist, no less, and possess a great deal of spirit. It, too, is real spirit after all, even if it has lost its way. Of course this lost spirit need not be presented as something very valuable. But having got lost, deluding itself that it considers matter to be the only reality, it is still filled with more spirit than the kind of unimaginative absence of anything spiritual at all which seeks the spirit by material means because it cannot find any trace of spirit within itself.

When you look back, therefore, at the beginnings, you have to understand the problematic way, if I may use the term, with which the revelations of the spiritual world entered the physical world in the last third of the nineteenth century. Those beginnings have, on the one hand, to be properly understood if the whole meaning and the circumstances governing the existence of the movement are to make sense. You need to understand how immature people's judgement was in general to receive these spiritual revelations and, above all, how serious was the intention in certain circles not to allow anything which would truly lead to the spirit to enter the public domain. There can be no doubt that the appearance of Blavatsky was likely to jolt very many people who were not to be taken lightly. And that is indeed what happened. Those people who still preserved some powers of discrimination reached the conclusion that here there was something which spoke for itself. It was curious how it came into the world at this particular moment but it was something that spoke for itself. You only needed to apply your common sense and it spoke for itself. But there were nevertheless many people whose interests would not be served by allowing this kind of stimulus to flow into the world.

But now it was here, was here in the form of a person like Blavatsky who, in a sense, handled her own inner revelation in a naive and helpless manner. That is already evident in the style of her writings. This is the way it was here; this is the way she handled it herself, naive and helpless in a certain sense and influenced by much that was happening around her. Indeed, do not believe that there was any difficulty—particularly with HP Blavatsky there was no great difficulty—for those who wanted to ensure that the world should not accept anything of a spiritual nature to attach themselves to her entourage. In a sense she was gullible because of her naive and helpless attitude to her own inner revelations. In the affair with the sliding doors, for example, through which the alleged Mahatma Letters were inserted, but which were written outside by ...[46] or some other person and inserted, it did not need HP Blavatsky first to tell ... to insert the letters but she was naive again in a certain sense, believed in such letters herself. The person who pushed them in deceived Blavatsky and the world. Then, of course, it was very easy to tell the world that she was a fraud. But do you not understand, my dear friends, that Blavatsky herself could have been deceived? For she was prone to an extraordinary gullibility precisely because of the special lack of hardness, as I would describe it, of her brain.

The problem is an exceedingly complicated one and demands, like everything of a true spiritual nature which enters the world in our time, power of judgement, a healthy common sense. It is not exactly evidence of healthy common sense to judge Adalbert Stifter incapable of becoming a teacher and subsequently, when the nod came—in this case it was again due to a woman, and probably one with a less sclerotic brain than all those officials in the ministries or the school commissions—to find him suitable to inspect all those he had not been allowed to join.

A healthy common sense is required to understand what is right. But there are some peculiar views about this healthy common sense. When I gave a bigger lecture cycle in Germany last year, I often referred to healthy common sense and added that what anthroposophy had to say from out of the spiritual world could be tested by healthy common sense. One of my critics, who was by no means the worst, even picked this up and found the following. He said almost verbatim that it was a wild-goose chase to talk about healthy common sense, because everyone with a scientific education knew that common sense which was healthy knows next to nothing, and anybody who claimed to know anything was not healthy. That was the content of a critical judgement which was even written in quite a witty style.

So, translated into more popular language, it means: if someone today, after a corresponding amount of human progress has happened, is clever, they know that we don't know anything; if they think they know something, they are mad. That is the stage we have reached in our receptivity to things spiritual.

Having thus presented you with some things from the time before the beginning of the anthroposophical movement with regard to the ability to receive a spiritual revelation, and having now presented you with the judgement of a not insignificant critic from as recently as last year, you can approximately see how contemporary attitudes have affected the whole movement. For it is almost inevitable—particularly given someone as difficult to understand as Blavatsky, whom people could point to—that in such a contemporary atmosphere the judgement should come about which basically is repeated in many variations, one person putting it like this, another like that: any clever person today, anyone with healthy common sense, will say *ignorabimus*; anyone who does not say *ignorabimus* must be either mad or a swindler.

We should not understand this only as something malicious. If we really want to understand our times in order to gain some insight into the conditions governing the existence of the anthroposophical movement, this must not be seen purely as the malicious intent of a few individuals. It has to be seen as something which in all countries, in contemporary humanity, belongs to the flavour of our times. We have to see through it as such. Then, however, we will be able to imbue the strong and courageous stand we should adopt with something which, if we look at our age from an anthroposophical point of view, should not be omitted—despite the decisive, spiritually decisive, rejection of our opponents' position. That is compassion. It is necessary to have compassion in spite of everything, because the clarity of judgement in our times has been obscured.

How the anthroposophical movement fared and had to fare because of the way things are is something we will talk about tomorrow.

# LECTURE FOUR

## DORNACH, 13 JUNE 1923

IF we look at a phenomenon such as HP Blavatsky, and if we do so from the perspective which will have become clear to you from our previous three reflections, we need on the one hand of course to be concerned first with her personality as such, looked at in its own right. The other aspect is the impact she had on a large number of people. Now it is true, of course, that this impact was in part quite negative. It would be true to say that those who came across Blavatsky's publications in so far as they had a, let us say, philosophical, psychological, literary, scientific—we could also say in general in the sense that the term is used today, a well-edu-cated—bent were glad to be rid of this phenomenon in one way or another, not to have to make a judgement of any kind. They could achieve this goal also simply by saying that she had engaged in dishonest practices and that there was no need to spend time on something where there was evidence, as people said, of that sort of thing.

Then there were those who were in possession of ancient, tradi-tional wisdom—a possession of which I told you yesterday how little they actually understood it, but used it in one way or another as an instrument of power—members of one or another secret society. We must never forget that numerous events in the world are linked to actions from such secret societies. They were not only glad not to have to make a judgement but were concerned above all to do every-thing possible to find a way to prevent such a depiction of the spir-itual world having a wider impact. Because, as we saw, these things had been published, they could be read by everyone, promulgated by everyone. And in this way the secret societies had been deprived of a good deal of the power which they wanted to preserve for them-selves. That is why it is of course members of such societies who are behind the things I characterized yesterday, namely the judgement that there were dishonest practices.

More important for our present purpose, however, is that Blav-atsky's writings and everything else connected with her personality made a certain impression on a large number of people. That led to the establishment of movements which describe themselves in one way or another as theosophical.

I would like you to remember that in these discussions I always try to present my material in such a way that it should correspond to the facts. This becomes impossible nowadays in many circles, simply because of the terminology that has to be used. What happens today is that when a person encounters a word it is very tempting for them to seek a dictionary definition in order to avoid having to look at the issue itself. When such a literary type, or indeed people who are taken more seriously than literary types, hear of theosophy they open a dictionary—which may well be a dictionary in their minds—and look up the word. Or perhaps they are much more conscientious and study all kinds of literature in which a word like theosophy occurs, and then use that as the basis for their judgement. In the writings that deal with such things, you have to be aware how much actually depends on this kind of procedure.

This must always be juxtaposed with the question: How did the society, or the societies, we might say, which base themselves on Blavatsky come to use the name Theosophical Society? Whatever you have against the Theosophical Society—and I listed a number of things one might have against it—one thing which did not hap-pen, when it was founded at the end of the nineteenth century, was to found a Theosophical Society with the aim of propagating the-osophy as defined in the dictionary. That was not the case at all. But a body of knowledge about the spiritual world existed through Blavatsky which initially was simply there as such. Then it was found necessary, for reasons that I still intend to discuss, to cultivate this knowledge through a society and a society requires a name. Then the people who were debating what name it should have—there is, after all, debate about everything today, there was debate about everything at that time too—asked themselves: Should it be called the New Mystical Society, should it be called the Rosicrucian Society, should it be called the Magic Society? And then they looked up what other words there were and arrived at the word theosophy and theosophical.

So the word really doesn't have anything much to do with what spread from there, insofar as it is a historically derived word. Therefore it is rather nonsensical to discuss things in terms of the meaning of the word, love it or hate it. It is a question of quite definite, concrete things which entered the world through the writings or other communications of Blavatsky. And it is, we might say, pure coincidence that the societies which came together called themselves the Theosophical Society. No one could think of a better word. This has to be clearly remembered because there exist of course not just historical judgements but also historical feelings. People who have learnt about the historical development of their given area of study are likely to have come across the term theosophy. But the term they have come across has nothing to do with what called itself the Theosophical Society.

Within the Anthroposophical Society, at any rate, such things ought to be taken very seriously. There should be a certain drive for accuracy, so that a proper feeling can develop for the subjective scribblings to which these things have gradually given rise.

But there is one question which should particularly concern us: Why is it that a large number of our contemporaries have felt the urge to follow up these revelations? Because that will provide us with the bridge to something of a quite different nature: to the Anthroposophical Society.

However, in considering the phenomenon of Blavatsky, it is important to highlight one characteristic of this personality in particular; because it stands out that HP Blavatsky had the characteristic, it would be true to say, of possessing wholly anti-Christian sentiments, possessing a wholly anti-Christian outlook. In her *Secret Doctrine* she revealed in one large sweep the differing impulses and development of the many ancient religions and the development of the religions. But she was simply not capable of an objective account. Everything which might have been expected as an objective account is clouded by her subjective judgement, the judgement of her feelings. She not only made judgements but demonstrated everywhere that she had a deep sympathy for every religion in the world that wasn't Judaism and Christianity and a deep antipathy for Judaism and Christianity. Blavatsky depicts everything which comes from the latter as inferior to the great revelations of the various pagan religions: in other words, an expressly anti-Christian outlook, but an expressly spiritual one.

She was able to speak of spiritual beings and spiritual processes in the same way that one normally speaks of the beings and processes of the physical world; she was able to discuss aspects of this spiritual world because she had the capacity to move among spiritual forces in the same way that contemporary people normally move among the forces of the physical senses. Blavatsky speaks of spiritual phenomena with the same sense of reality as people speak of things in the physical world. In other words, an expressly spiritual outlook and an expressly anti-Christian outlook.

But that gives her the additional ability to bring to the surface and clarify characteristic impulses of the various pantheistic religions.

Now we might be surprised by two things. First, that it is possible at all for someone to appear today—I mean 'today' of course in a historical sense—who has such an anti-Christian outlook and expects the salvation of humanity to come from this anti-Christian outlook. And second, we might be surprised—given that outwardly hardly anyone has a heathen outlook but that outwardly the people, at least in our civilized regions, have a Jewish or Christian outlook—that nevertheless there was a decisive and profound influence exerted specifically on people with a Christian outlook—less so perhaps on those with a Jewish background. These are two questions we must ponder when we speak about conditions governing the existence of the contemporary life of the spirit among the broader masses in general.

Now in respect of Blavatsky's anti-Christian perspective, I want only to remind people that someone who became much better known than she in Central Europe, among certain circles at least, had as much of an anti-Christian perspective as Blavatsky. That was Nietzsche.[47] It is difficult to be more anti-Christian than the author of *The Anti-Christ*. As dissimilar as Nietzsche is to Blavatsky—even if only that Blavatsky was a more or less uneducated woman in terms of what is now called modern education, whereas Nietzsche was highly educated—as dissimilar as they were otherwise in the whole attitude of their souls, they did show a strange similarity in that they are eminently anti-Christian in orientation. It would be adopting a very superficial attitude not to enquire into the reason for the anti-Christian outlook of these two personalities. But to find an answer one needs to dig a little bit deeper.

For we need to have a clear understanding that people today, indeed increasing numbers of people today are becoming divided in their spiritual life, something which they do not always acknowledge and which they try to paper over with a certain intellectual cowardice, but which is all the more active in the unconscious depths of their mind.

One needs to have a clear understanding of the way in which the European peoples and their American cousins have been influenced by the educational endeavours of the last three, four, five hundred years. One need only consider how great the difference really is between the content of today's secular education and the religious impulses of humanity. It is true, after all, that most people are prone to the most terrible illusions in this respect. From the time people enter elementary school all thinking, their whole inner orientation, is directed toward this modern education. Then they are also provided with what is meant to satisfy their religious needs. A dreadful gap opens up between the two. People never really have the opportunity to deal inwardly with this chasm; they don't have the opportunity, preferring instead to submit to the most dreadful illusions in this respect.

This raises questions about the historical process which led to the creation of this yawning chasm. For this we have to look back to those centuries in which such modern education did not yet exist, in which learning was the province of those few who were thoroughly prepared for it. You can be quite certain that a twelve-year-old schoolgirl today has a greater fund of worldly knowledge than any educated person of the eleventh, twelfth or thirteenth centuries. These things must not be overlooked. Education has come to rely on an extraordinarily intense feeling of authority, an almost invincible sense of authority. In the course of the centuries, this education has, we might say, become more and more dependent on something that makes this belief in authority in modern education greater and greater. In the course of the centuries modern education has increasingly comprised only the knowledge of what can be demonstrated to the outer senses, or by calculation.

Well, the less a person considers these things inwardly, the more obvious it appears to them that what we see with our five senses, as they say, and what we see as being calculated in the same way that two times two equals four, is true. What you see with your five senses, which is the same as two times two equalling four, that is true. By denying everything else and in the end increasingly only including in modern education what is as true as what we see with the five senses or can count with our five fingers, such 'two times two equals four' gradually equipped modern education with the sense of authority that it has—because it has such great authority, this 'two times two is four' and these five senses, because we can say of such authority that it has the same certainty as that two times two equals four, and as what the five senses say.

But that also increasingly gave rise to the feeling that everything which human beings believe, which they consider to be right, has to justify itself before the certainty of modern learning. And because such modern education was increasingly focused on the senses and what can be calculated, it was impossible to ever present to people in an appropriate way any truth from those realms where mathematics no longer applies and where the senses no longer apply. How were these truths presented to humanity in earlier centuries prior to the existence of modern learning?

They were presented in ritual images. The essential element in the spread of religion over the centuries lay not in the sermons, for instance, but in ceremonial, in the rituals. It was clear that one could not speak through the intellect which was not yet developed in the

way it is today but that one had to speak through the image. Try
to imagine for a moment what it was like in Christian countries in
the fourteenth or fifteenth centuries. There the sermon was not the
main thing; the main thing was the ceremonial. The main thing was
for people to enter a world presented to them in mighty and gran-
diose images. All around, frescoes on the walls reminded them of
the spiritual life. It was as if their earthly life could reach as high
as the tallest mountain, but at that point, if one could climb just a
little bit higher, the spiritual life began. The language of the spiritual
world was depicted in images which stimulated the imagination, in
the audible harmonies of music, or in the words of set forms such as
mantras and prayers. Those times understood clearly that images, not
concepts, were required for the spiritual world. People needed something vividly pictorial not something which could be debated. Something was required which would allow the spirit to speak through
what was accessible to the senses.

Then modern education arose with its intellectual aspirations, with
its aspiration to justify everything by reason, as people say. Christianity, too, the Christian mysteries, the Mystery of Golgotha and everything connected with it, were essentially spoken about in the form
of images, even when words were used in story form. And when
the dogmas emerged, they were also still understood as something
pictorial. So we can say: Until the thirteenth, fourteenth century, the
Christian message was absolutely proclaimed in the old way. And this
Christian message remained unchallenged from any quarter prior to
the existence of intellectual learning, and for as long as these things
did not have to be justified by reason.

Now just look at historical processes in the thirteenth, fourteenth,
fifteenth and sixteenth centuries, the urgency with which human
beings begin to experience the drive to understand everything intel-
lectually. People today usually no longer appreciated how this introduced a critical attitude of world-historical significance.

Thus we can say that people today—and this really is not just the
people in the top ten thousand but the broad spectrum of people—
are introduced to religious life through Christianity but alongside that
to modern learning also. As a consequence, the two—Christianity

and modern learning—coexist in each soul. And even if people do not realize it, it transpires that the results of intellectual education cannot be used to prove Christian truths. The Christian truths cannot be proved with it. So from childhood people are now taught the fact that two times two equals four and that the five senses must only be used in such a context. They are taught this certainty and realize, if they want to adhere to such certainty, that Christianity cannot be made compatible with it after all.

Those theologians, modern theologians who have tried to marry the two have lost Christ, are no longer able to speak to the broad spectrum of people about Christ; at most they speak about the personality of Jesus. Thus Christianity itself has been able to be preserved in recent centuries only in its old forms. But modern people are simply no longer willing to accept this in their souls; it no longer has a firm base in the soul. Why?

Well, just look at the way Christianity has developed historically. It is extremely dishonest when theologians today try to interpret Christianity with rationalism in any way. It is impossible to interpret Christianity rationalistically. Christianity, the Mystery of Golgotha and everything connected with it cannot be interpreted rationalistically; we have to talk about spirituality if we want to speak about Christ. We have to speak of a spiritual world if we want to talk about Christ. It is not possible to believe only in what is absolutely certain, that two time two equals four, to believe in one's five senses, and then continue to speak about Christ in an honest way. That is simply not possible, so that in their innermost soul modern human beings did not have the means to understand Christ on the basis of what they had been taught at school. For rationalism and intellectualism have robbed them of the spiritual world. Christ is still present in name and tradition, but the feeling for what that means is gone; the understanding of Christ as a spiritual being among spiritual beings in a spiritual world has disappeared. The world created by modern astronomy, biology and science is a world devoid of spirit.

Thus numerous souls grew up who, for these reasons, had quite specific needs. Time really does progress, and the people of today, I have often emphasized this, are not the same as people in earlier ages. You must have said to yourselves: I meet here with a certain number of others in a society to cultivate spiritual truths. Why do I do that? Why do you, each single one of you, do that? What drives you to do that? Well, the thing which drives people to do this is usually so deeply embedded in the unconscious depths of their soul life that there is little clarity about it. But here, where we want to reflect on our position as anthroposophists, as I just said in the introduction, the question has to be asked.

If you look back to earlier times, it was self-evident to people that it was not just material things and processes out there but that spirits were everywhere. People perceived a spiritual world which surrounded them in their environment. And because they found a spiritual world they were able to understand Christ.

Modern intellectualism makes it impossible to discover a spiritual world, if we are honest, and as a consequence it is impossible to understand Christ properly. And the modern educated person does not understand Christ. The people who try so hard to rediscover a spiritual life are very specific souls. They are the souls driven by two things. Really, in most of the souls who come together in societies such as the ones we are talking about here there live two things today. First, a vague feeling appears in the soul that people cannot describe but which is there. And if this feeling is investigated with the means available in the spiritual world it turns out to be a feeling which stems from earlier lives on earth in which a spiritual environment still existed. Today, people are appearing in whose souls something from their previous lives on earth remains active. There would be neither theosophists nor anthroposophists if such people did not exist in whom something from previous lives on earth remains active. They are to be found in all sections of society. They do not know that their feeling is the result of earlier lives on earth, but it is. And it makes them search for a very specific path, for very specific knowledge.

Indeed, my dear friends, the way you saw the trees in earlier earth lives, the way you saw the outer material substances, has no effect on this present earth life, for you saw that with your senses. The senses have atomized in the cosmos. What continues to have an effect is the spiritual content of earlier lives on earth.

Human beings today are affected in two ways. They can have the feeling that there is something within them—they don't know that it comes from previous lives on earth, but it does come from previous lives on earth—which affects them, which is simply there. But even though they might know a great deal about the physical world they cannot describe this feeling because nothing which was not of a spiritual nature has been carried over. If, however, in the present I am deprived of everything spiritual, then what has come over from a previous life remains dissatisfied. That is the one aspect.

The other effect which lives in human beings is a vague feeling that their dreams should really reveal more than the sensory world. It is of course an error, an illusion if people believe that their dreams should reveal more than the sensory world. But what is the origin of this illusion, which has arisen in parallel with the development of modern learning? Because there is something peculiar about this modern learning. When people who have had the benefit of a modern education gather together in their learned circles they have to show their cultural breeding, then people talk in the way that people do who have been educated in a modern sense. If someone starts to talk about spiritual effects in the world people adopt an air of ridicule, because that is what being cultured demands. It is not acceptable within our school education to talk about spiritual effects in the world. To do so implies superstition, lack of education. Then you have to adopt an air of ridicule. Then you have to show that something like that is only for the superstitious part of the population.

Two groups will then often form in such circles. Frequently someone plucks up a little courage to talk about spiritual things. People then adopt an air of ridicule. The majority leave to play cards or indulge in some other worthy pursuit. But a few are intrigued. They go into a another room and begin to talk about these things while the others play cards or do something else which I don't need to describe here. The people in the other room listen with open mouths and cannot get enough of it; but it has to be in a separate room because anything else shows a lack of education. The things which a modern person can learn there are more or less dream-like. The things which are told there are mostly as incoherent and chaotic as dreaming, but people love it all the same. Why do they love it? Those who have gone to play cards would also love it, except that their passion for cards is even stronger. At least that is what they tell themselves.

Why do human beings in our modern age feel the urge to investigate their dreams? Because they feel quite instinctively, without any clear understanding: the content of my thoughts and what I see depicted in the physical world is all very nice, but it does not give me anything for my soul life. Something else lies behind it; I can feel that within me. A secret thinking, feeling and willing lives in me when I am awake which is as free as my dream life is free when I am sleeping. There is something in the depths of the soul which is dreamt even when awake. Modern people feel that. And they feel it precisely because the spiritual element is missing from the physical world. They can only catch a glimpse of it when they are dreaming. In earlier lives on earth they saw it in everything around them.

And now those souls are being born who can feel working within themselves not only impulses from their previous lives on earth, but what took place in the spiritual world in their pre-earthly existence. This is related to their internal dreaming. It is an echo of life before birth.

Just think, people in earlier times knew about the spirit surrounding them; their earthly existence did not deprive them of the spirit, as it were. Modern people feel the spirit within themselves. But not only does the soul constitution of the time deny them the spirit; an educational system has arisen which is hostile to the spirit, which proves the spirit out of existence.

If we ask how people found a common interest in such societies as we are describing here, it is through these two features of the soul; namely, that something is active both from their previous earth lives and from their pre-earthly existence. This is the case for most of you. You would not be sitting here if these two things were not active in you.

And think back to earlier social conditions. In very ancient times social institutions had their origin in the mysteries, and were in harmony with the content of their spiritual teaching.

Take an Athenian for example. He revered the goddess Athena. He was part of a social community which he knew to be constituted according to Athena's intentions. The olive trees around Athens were planted by her. The laws of the state had been dictated by her. Human beings were part of a social community which was in total accord with their inner beliefs. Nothing the gods had given them had, as it were, been taken away.

Compare that with modern human beings. They are placed in a social context in which there is a huge gap between their inner experiences and the way they are integrated into society. It feels to them as if their souls are divorced from their bodies by social circumstances, only they are not aware of it; it is embedded in the subconscious. Through these characteristics, through these impulses from earlier lives on earth and pre-earthly existence I referred to, people feel connected with a spiritual world. Their bodies belong to the outer institutions. Their bodies have to behave in a way that will satisfy social institutions. It provokes a persistent subconscious fear that their physical bodies no longer really belong to them. Well, there are modern states in which one feels that your clothes no longer belong to you because the tax man is after them! But, you see, in a larger context, my dear friends, a person's physical body is no longer their property either. It is claimed by society.

This is the fear which lives in modern human beings, that every day they have to give up their bodies to something which is not connected with their souls. And so modern people become seekers after something which belongs to quite different ages, which they experienced in previous lives on earth. So modern people become seekers after something which does not belong to the earth, which belongs to the spiritual world, and in which they were in their pre-earthly existence.

All this takes its effect unconsciously, instinctively, but it takes effect. And it has to be said that the Anthroposophical Society as it has developed had its origins in small beginnings. To begin with, it had to work in the most basic way with very small groups, and there is much to be said about the ways and means in which work took place in such small groups.

For example, in the first years in Berlin I had to lecture in a room in which beer glasses were clinking in the background because it was a barroom which went out to the street. And once, when it was not available, we were shown into something not unlike a stable. The people came there who were, who are, as I have just described. In one German town I lectured in a hall, parts of which had no floor, where one had to be careful not to tumble into a hole and break a leg. But that is where people gathered who felt these impulses. Indeed, this movement aimed to be universally human, right from the beginning. Thus the satisfaction was just as great when the simplest mind turned up in such locations as I have just described. At the same time it was no great worry when people came together in order to launch the anthroposophical movement in more aristocratic fashion, as happened in Munich, because that, too, was part of humanity. No aspect of humanity was excluded.

But the important point, my dear friends, was that the souls who met in this way always had the qualities I have described. So that the people who came together in such societies were really marked by destiny, and are still marked by destiny today.

If such people had not existed, then someone like Blavatsky would not have engendered any interest, because it was among such people that she made her mark. What did these people feel to begin with? What was most important to them and what corresponded to their sentiments?

Well, the concept of reincarnation corresponded to one of the things which was active in their souls. Now they could see themselves straddling the ages as human beings, making them stronger than the forces which daily tried to rob them of their bodies. The response to this deep-seated, almost will-like, inner feeling of human beings had to be the teaching of reincarnation.

And the dreamlike, out-of-body experience of the soul, which even the simplest country person can experience, could never be satisfied with knowledge which was based only on matter and its processes. For within matter and its processes there was nothing similar to what a person experienced in their soul, which was an echo of their pre-earthly existence. That could only be responded to by making it clear to them that the most profound aspect of human nature exists as if it is woven out of dreams, if I may put it in this radical way. Those things that are woven in the same way that dreams are woven, but which have a stronger reality, a stronger existence, they are not the same as the things in our physical environment. We are like fish out of water if we are forced to live our soul life in the world which has been conjured up for people by modern education. In the same way that fish cannot exist in air and begin to gasp, so our souls live in the contemporary environment, gasping for what they need. They fail to find it, because it is spiritual in nature; because it is the echo of their experiences in life before birth in the spiritual world. They want to hear about the spirit, that the spirit exists, that the spirit is right in our midst.

You have to understand that these were the two most important concerns for a certain section of humanity: learning that human beings live more than a single life on earth, and learning that among the natural things and processes there are beings in the world like themselves, spiritual beings. It was Blavatsky who initially brought this. It was necessary to possess that knowledge before it was possible to understand Christ once again.

As far as Blavatsky was concerned, however—and in saying this we should emphasize her compassion for humanity—she realized that these people were gasping for knowledge of the spiritual world, and she thought that she would meet their spiritual needs by revealing the ancient pagan religions to them. That was to be done first.

It is quite easy to understand that this had to result in a tremendously one-sided anti-Christian standpoint, just as it is easy to understand that Nietzsche's observation of Christianity in its present form, which he had outgrown, led him to adopt such a strong anti-Christian attitude.

This anti-Christian outlook, and how it might be healed, is the topic I want to address in the next lectures. It remains only to emphasize that what appeared with Blavatsky as an anti-Christian standpoint was absent right from the beginning in the anthroposophical movement, because the first lecture cycle which I gave was 'From Buddha to Christ'. Thus the anthroposophical movement takes an independent position within all these spiritual movements in that, from the start, it pursued a path from the pagan religions to Christianity. But it is equally necessary to understand why others did not follow this path. That is what we will talk about tomorrow.

# LECTURE FIVE

## DORNACH, 14 JUNE 1923

I T is important to be aware of the need which existed in the anthroposophical movement for Christianity to be won specifically among those who were initially what might be described as ordinary listeners. For the theosophical movement under the guidance of HP Blavatsky had adopted an expressly anti-Christian orientation. I wish to start by throwing a little more light on this anti-Christian attitude, a perspective which I also mentioned in connection with Friedrich Nietzsche.

It has to be understood, and this is clear from a great variety of reflections, that the Mystery of Golgotha occurred in the first instance simply as a fact in the development of humanity on earth. In the first instance it simply has to be taken as a fact. If you look at the way in which I have dealt with the subject in my book, *Christianity As Mystical Fact*, you will find that I attempted to come to an understanding of the impulses underlying the ancient mysteries, and then to show how the various forces which were active in the individual mystery centres were harmonized and unified. Thus what was initially encountered by human beings in a hidden way could be presented openly as a historical fact. In this sense the historical reality of the Mystery of Golgotha represents the culmination of the ancient mysteries. How then the whole development of humanity had to change under the influence of the Mystery of Golgotha, that is precisely what I tried to show in that book.

Now, as I have often emphasized previously, remnants of the ancient mystery wisdom were present when the Mystery of Golgotha took place as a fact. With the aid of these remnants which were incorporated into the Gospels, as I set out in that book, it was possible to find access to this event, which actually gave earth development its true meaning. The means of understanding the Mystery of Golgotha could be taken from the ancient mysteries. But at the same time it must be recorded that the mystery system, in the sense in which it existed in ancient times, was disappearing and found its culmination in the Mystery of Golgotha.

And I also mentioned that the impulses derived from ancient wisdom which were still directly experienced began to fade in the fourth century AD, so that the wisdom was preserved more or less only in the form of tradition, allowing particular people in one place or another to revitalize these traditions. But the kind of continuous development which the mysteries enjoyed in ancient times had disappeared, taking with it the means to understand the Mystery of Golgotha.

The tradition remained. The Gospels existed, kept secret at first by the communities of the Church and then made public for individual peoples. The cults existed. As the Western world developed it was possible to keep alive some form of memory of the Mystery of Golgotha. But the opportunity to maintain the memory came to an end in that moment in the fifth post-Atlantean epoch when intellectualism, with what I described yesterday as modern education, made its appearance. And with it a type of science of the natural world began which pre-empted any understanding of the spiritual world as it developed the kind of methodology it has done so far. This methodology needed to be expanded in the way that anthroposophy has sought to do. But if there was no progression beyond the scientific method introduced by Copernicus, Galileo and so on, the Mystery of Golgotha had no place within such a view of nature.

Now consider the following. In none of the ancient religions was there any division between knowledge of the natural world and, let us say, knowledge of God. Secular, profane science led over into theology in a completely natural way. It is a common feature of all pagan religions that there is a unity in the way in which they explain nature and in how that understanding of nature then ascends to an understanding of the divine, the many-faceted divinity, which is active in nature.

The kind of abstract natural forces we have today, unchallenged in their absoluteness, did not exist. What did exist were nature spirits which guided the various aspects of nature, and with which links could be established through the content of the human soul. So that nowhere in the old religions was there that rift which exists between that which is modern natural science and that which is supposed to be the understanding of the divine-spiritual.

Now anthroposophy will never make the claim that it somehow intends to establish a religion. On the other hand, although religion will always need to be an independent spiritual stream in humanity, it is simply a human demand that there should be harmony between that which is cognition and that which is religion. It must be possible to make the transition from cognition to religion and to return from religion to cognition without having to cross an abyss. That is impossible, given the structure of modern cognition. And such cognition has become very popular and subjugates people with tremendous authority. As things are, a bridge between such cognition and the religious life is impossible; above all, it is impossible to discover the nature of Christ on this scientific basis. Modern science, in investigating the being of Christ ever more closely, has scattered and lost it.

If you bear this in mind, you will be able to understand what follows. Let me begin by talking about Nietzsche, far removed from Blavatsky. In Nietzsche we have a person who grew up in a Central European Protestant parsonage, the son not only of pious people in the modern sense, but the son of a practising minister. He went through a modern academic school education. But since he was not what Schiller called a bread-and-butter scholar but a thinker—as you know, Schiller made a sharp distinction in his inaugural speech[48] between a thinker and a bread-and-butter scholar—his interest extended to everything which could be learnt through modern methods. So he consciously and in a radical way became aware of the dichotomy which in reality affects all modern minds, although people do not realize it and are prone to illusion because they draw a veil over it. A mood develops in him which I would like to characterize roughly as follows.

He says: Here we have a modern learning. Nowhere does modern learning provide a direct link to an explanation of Jesus Christ without jumping over an abyss. Now what has remained as Christianity inserts itself into what modern learning has become; Christianity which speaks in words that no longer bear any relation at all to the various formulations, characterizations that come from modern science. His uncompromising conclusion is that if we want to establish a relationship with modern science while preserving some sort of inner feeling for the traditional explanations of Christ, it is necessary to lie. That is his conclusion. And so he chooses. He chooses modern learning—and thus arrives at a radical indictment of what he knew about Christianity.

No one has been more cutting about Christianity than Nietzsche, the minister's son. And he experiences this, let me say, with his whole being. One example is when he says—I am only quoting him, I do not, of course, advocate what Nietzsche said, but I am quoting him—that what a modern theologian believes to be true is certainly false. Indeed, one can virtually make it a criterion of truth: we recognize in Nietzsche's sense what is false if a modern theologian calls it true. That is roughly his definition, one of his definitions of truth. And he finds that the whole of modern philosophy has too much theological blood flowing through its veins. As a result he formulates his tremendous indictment of Christianity, which is of course blasphemous, but which is an honest blasphemy and therefore worthy of greater attention than the hypocrisy which is so often found in this field today. It needs to be emphasized that a person like Nietzsche, who was serious about wanting to understand the Mystery of Golgotha, was not able to do so with the means at his disposal, including the Gospels in their present form.

Anthroposophy provides an interpretation of all four Gospels.[49] What the Gospels become through this interpretation is rejected decisively by theologians of all denominations. But it was not yet available to Nietzsche. It is the most difficult thing for a scientific mind—and almost all people today have scientific minds in this sense, even if at a basic level—to come to terms with the Mystery of Golgotha. Because what does that require? To come to terms with the Mystery of Golgotha in particular requires not a renewal of the old mysteries but the discovery of a whole new mystery knowledge. What is necessary is the discovery of the spiritual world in a wholly new form. For with the old mysteries, including gnosis, it was only possible to stutter about the Mystery of Golgotha. It was understood in a stuttering way. And today we must turn this stuttering into speech.

This urge to turn the old stuttering into speech—that is precisely what the many homeless souls had whom I refer to in these reflections. Nietzsche produced a radically formulated, not only rejection, but terrible indictment of Christianity. Basically Blavatsky's inspiration also came from the ancient mysteries. If we take *The Secret Doctrine* as a whole, it really feels like nothing fundamentally new but the resurrection of that knowledge which was used in the ancient mysteries to recognize the divine and the spiritual. The most important thing that emerges in Blavatsky's works is precisely the resurrection of the ancient mysteries, the resurrection of those insights through which the divine-spiritual was recognized in the ancient mysteries.

But these mysteries are only capable of explaining the events which happened in preparation of Christ. Those who were still familiar in a certain way with the impulses of the ancient mysteries when Christianity was still young were able to adopt a positive attitude to what happened at Golgotha. So that people were still able to adopt a positive attitude to what happened at Golgotha into the fourth century. The Greek Church Fathers were still understood in the real sense; how they were connected everywhere with the ancient mysteries, and how their words had quite a different tone from those of the later Latin Church Fathers.

It was that ancient wisdom which understood nature and spirit as one which was contained in Blavatsky's revelations. And in the way that a soul might be described as looking at nature and spirit before the Mystery of Golgotha, so, in turn, did Blavatsky. That is the way, she thought, to find the divine and the spiritual, to make them accessible to human perception. And from that perspective she turned her attention to what present-day traditional thinking and the modern faiths were saying about Jesus Christ. She could not, of course, understand the Gospels in the way they are understood in anthroposophy, and the knowledge which came from elsewhere was not adequate to deal with the knowledge of the spirit which Blavatsky brought. Hence her contempt for the way in which the Mystery of Golgotha was understood by the world out there. In her view, what people were saying about the Mystery of Golgotha was on a much lower level than all the majestic wisdom provided by the ancient mysteries. In other words, the Christian God stands on a lower level than the content of the ancient mysteries.

That was not the fault of the Christian God, but it was the result of interpretations of the Christian God. Blavatsky simply did not know the nature of the Mystery of Golgotha and was able to judge it only by what was being said about it. These things have to be seen in an objective light. As the power of the ancient mysteries was drawing to a final close in the last remnants of Greek culture in the fourth century AD, Rome took possession of Christianity. Roman culture was incapable of opening a real path to the spirit out of its external learning. Roman culture forced Christianity to adopt its outer trappings. It is this romanized Christianity alone which was known to Nietzsche and Blavatsky.

Thus we have to understand that these souls whom I described as homeless, whose earlier earth lives were lighting up within them, took the first thing on offer. Their sole aim was to find access to the spiritual world, even at the risk of losing Christianity. These people wanted a connection between the soul and the spirit. So those people were encountered who began by seeking a way into the Theosophical Society.

Now the position of anthroposophy in relation to these people, these homeless souls, has to be clearly understood. After all, these were searching souls, these were questioning souls. And the first necessity was to find out what questions resided in their innermost selves. And if anthroposophy addressed these souls, it was because they had questions about things to which anthroposophy thought it had the answer. The other people among our contemporaries don't have questions; they lack the questions.

Anthroposophy thus did not have the task of seeking knowledge among the theosophists. As a starting point, it considered what came into the world with Blavatsky to be an important fact. But its purpose was not to observe the knowledge which she presented, but essentially the necessity to understand those questions, those puzzles which existed in a number of souls.

If there had been any possibility at all at that time to express the matter clearly, we might have said: We need not concern ourselves with what has been given to people by the leaders of the Theosophical Society, that need not concern us, but we must concern ourselves with what souls are asking, what they want to know. That is why these people were nevertheless initially the right people for anthroposophy.

How were the answers to be formulated? We need to look at the matter as positively and as factually as possible. Here we had these questioning souls. Their questions were clear. They believed they could find an answer to them in something like Annie Besant's book *The Ancient Wisdom*,[50] for instance. Obviously, it would have been stupid to tell people that this or that bit of *The Ancient Wisdom* was no longer relevant for our modern time because then you would not have offered anything to these souls but only taken something away. The only possible course was to give them real answers, whereas they did not receive any proper answers from the other side. I therefore introduced a real response by ignoring *The Ancient Wisdom* when this book was initially, as it were, dogma among these people, and by writing my book *Theosophy*,[51] which gave answers to questions which I knew were being asked. That was the positive answer. And there was no need to do more than that. People had to be left completely free to choose whether they wanted to pick up *The Ancient Wisdom* or whether they wanted to pick up *Theosophy*.

In times of great historical change things are not decided in as rational and direct a manner as we normally like to think. Thus I did not find it at all surprising that the theosophists who attended the lecture cycle on anthroposophy when the German Section was established remarked, as I already pointed out to you in these reflections, that it did not agree in the slightest with what Mrs Besant was saying.

Of course it could not agree, because the answers had to be found in what the consciousness, the deepened consciousness of the present can provide. And so it happened, if I am to characterize to begin with what I might call the major threads, that initially until about 1907 each step taken by anthroposophy was a battle against the traditions of the Theosophical Society. At first the members of the Theosophical Society were the only people whom one could approach with these things. Every step had to be conquered. A polemical approach would have been useless; the only sensible course was hope, and making the right choices.

These things certainly did not happen without inner reservations. Everything had to be done at the right time and place, at least in my view. I believe that in my *Theosophy* I did not go one step beyond what it was possible to publish for a certain number of people at that time. The wide distribution of the book since then shows that this was an accurate assumption. It was as far as I could go.

It was possible to go further among those who were engaged in a more intensive search, who had been caught up in the stream set in motion by Blavatsky. A start had to be made in going further. I could describe all of the individual examples. But I will single out only one instance; how the attempt was made to move step by step from the bad traditions into the proper present, into the results of direct research in the present.

It was common in the Theosophical Society to describe how human beings went through what was called Kamaloka after death. The description given by its leaders could only be sidestepped in my book *Theosophy* by, in the first instance, avoiding the concept of time. But within Society groups I wanted to deal with the correct concept of time.

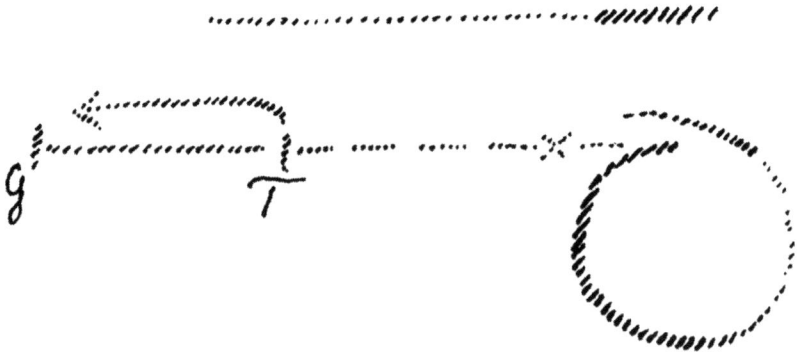

*G = birth　T = death*

As a result I gave various lectures about life between death and a new birth within the then Dutch Section of the Theosophical Society and there pointed out, right at the start of my activity, that it is nonsense simply to imagine that, if this is our earth life between birth and death, then we pass through Kamaloka as if our consciousness is merely extended a little (see diagram above).

I showed that time has to be seen as moving backwards, and I described how our existence in Kamaloka is life in reverse, stage by stage, only at three times the pace of ordinary earth life or as the life spent on earth.

Nowadays, of course, people leading their physical lives have no idea that this backward motion is a reality, a reality in the spiritual realm, because time is imagined simply as a straight line from start to finish and people today have no concept of its reverse motion.

Now the leaders of the Theosophical Society professed to renew the teachings of the old wisdom. Blavatsky's book was used to build on it. All kinds of other writings appeared which built on Blavatsky's book. But their content took a form which corresponded exactly to the way things are presented as a result of modern materialism. Why? Because new knowledge, not simply the renewal of old knowledge, had to be pursued if the right things were to be found. The same old stuff kept being quoted. Buddha's wheel of birth and death and the old oriental wisdom also kept being quoted. But that a wheel is not something that can be described as a straight line, that was ignored by people, and that a wheel can only be drawn if it turns back on itself (see diagram). There was no life in this rejuvenation of the old wisdom, because it did not spring from direct knowledge. In short, it was necessary through direct knowledge to create something which was also capable of illuminating the ancient wisdom.

Thus in the first seven years of anthroposophical work in particular, it happened that there were people—well, who were quite content that, as they described it, there was no renewal in the theosophical field. They said: What is told there is no different to everything else; the differences are immaterial. They were argued away. But people never forgot the trouble I caused in the Dutch Section at the time, right at the beginning of my work, by filling my lectures with life, not simply parroting dogmatically, like the others did, what was written in the dogmatic books of the Theosophical Society. Anyone who might still remember those periods of our development only has to think back to the congress which took place in Munich in 1907,[52] when we were still in the lap of the Theosophical Society, and the Dutch theosophists were seething that an alien influence, as they perceived it, was muscling in. They did not have a sense that something living was standing against something which was based merely on tradition, but they experienced it as something alien.

Something had to change. That is when the conversation between Mrs Besant and myself took place in Munich,[53] and it was clarified that the things which I had to represent, had to represent as anthroposophy, would work quite independently of other things active within the Theosophical Society. What I might describe as a modus vivendi was agreed.

On the other hand, even at that time the absurdities of the Theosophical Society, which eventually led to its downfall, began to be visible on the horizon. For we can say today that it has been ruined as a society which is able to support a spiritual movement, however many registered members it has. What the Theosophical Society used to be is no longer alive today.

We have to be very clear about this: when anthroposophy began its work, the Theosophical Society still contained a justified and full spirituality, even if it was traditional. The things which were brought into the world by Blavatsky were a reality, and people had a living relationship with them.

But Blavatsky had already been dead for a decade as far as her life on earth was concerned. We can only say that the mood within the Theosophical Society, the things which existed as a continuation of Blavatsky's work, had a solid foundation in cultural history; they were quite capable of giving something to people. But even at that time they nevertheless already contained certain seeds of decay. The only question was whether these seeds of decay could be overcome, or whether they would inevitably lead to complete disharmony between anthroposophy and the old Theosophical Society.

Now it has to be said that one of the streams which existed in the Theosophical Society even in Blavatsky's time was actually a terribly strong destructive element. It is simply necessary, if we want to look at the matter in the way as I am doing now, to separate what was lobbed into modern life as spiritual content by Blavatsky from the effect of the way in which she was prompted to make her revelations from out of herself in her characteristic way. For in the first place we have a personality in Blavatsky who was just as I have described her to you in the last few days; who simply, when prompted from some quarter, through treachery if you like, was nevertheless creative, as I said, and through herself gave wisdom to humanity in book form—even if it was as if in memory of earlier lives on earth and only as the rejuvenation of ancient wisdom. This second fact must be fully separated from the first, for this second fact, that Blavatsky was prompted in a particular way to act as she did, introduced elements into the theosophical movement which were no longer as they should have been if this theosophical movement was to become a purely spiritual movement.

For that it was not. The fact is that Blavatsky was prompted from a certain direction, which I do not want to speak about any further, and as a result produced the things which are written in *Isis Unveiled*. But by various machinations Blavatsky for a second time fell under the influence of Eastern occult teachers behind whom were cultural tendencies of an egoistic nature. From the beginning a one-sided Eastern policy lay at the basis of the things they wished to achieve by way of Blavatsky. There was a tendency in them to show the materialistic West the much greater value of the spiritual insights of the East compared to the materialism of the West. There was a tendency in them to create a kind of sphere of influence—first of a spiritual nature, but then in a more general sense—of the East over the West by providing the West's spirituality, or lack of it if you like, with Eastern wisdom. That is how the transformation took place from the thoroughly European nature of *Isis Unveiled* to the thoroughly Eastern nature of Blavatsky's *The Secret Doctrine*.

Various factors were at work. But one of these factors was the wish to link India with Asia in order to create an Indo-Asian sphere of influence with the help of the Russian Empire. In this way her teaching received its Indian content in order to win a spiritual victory over the West. You see, that is a one-sidedly egoistical, nationally egoistical influence. It was present right from the beginning and was striking in its symptomatic significance. The first lecture by Annie Besant which I attended dealt with theosophy and imperialism.[54] And if one wanted an answer to the question whether the fundamental impulse of this lecture lay in a continuation of Blavatsky's actual spiritual direction or whether the fundamental impulse of this lecture lay in a continuation of what went alongside it, the answer had to be the latter.

Annie Besant was the kind of person who frequently said things without fully understanding what ultimately lay behind them. She often put her back into things without understanding what ultimately lay behind them. The ultimate connections were unknown to her. But if you read the lecture 'Theosophy and Imperialism' attentively, with an awareness of the underlying implications, you will see that if someone wanted to separate India from England, in a certain sense separate it in a spiritual way, the first, an apparently innocuous step could be taken in a lecture of this kind.

It has always spelled the beginning of the end for such spiritual movements and societies when they start to introduce partisan political elements into their activity, whereas a spiritual movement can only develop in the world today if it embraces all humanity. Indeed, today it is one of the most essential conditions for a spiritual movement whose intention it is to give access to the real spirit that it should embrace all humanity. And anything which is not universally human, which aims to split humanity in any way is, from the beginning, a destructive element for a spiritual movement that is meant to guide us into the real spiritual world.

But just consider the extent to which such things reach into the subconscious regions of the human psyche. It is simply part of the conditions for spiritual movements, such as anthroposophy also wants to be, for example, that at minimum they honestly and seriously endeavour to distance themselves from all partisan human interests, and aspire to take account of the general interest of humanity. That was what made the theosophical movement so destructive, that from the beginning it contained such a divisive element. And on occasion such an element can also veer in its position: during the War there was a tendency to become very anglo-chauvinistic. But particularly in such a situation it is essential to understand very clearly that it is completely impossible to make a genuine spiritual movement flourish if it contains factional interests which people are unwilling to leave behind.

That is why the outer dangers facing the anthroposophical movement today—in an age deteriorating everywhere into nationalistic posturing—include, above all, the lack of courage among people to discard these nationalistic tendencies.

But what is the root cause of such one-sidedness? It arises when a society wants to accrue power by something other than spiritual revelation. It is indeed true to say that while there was still much that was positive in the way the Theosophical Society developed an awareness of its power at the turn of the nineteenth to the twentieth century, that had almost completely disappeared by 1906 and was replaced by a strong drive for power.

It is important to understand properly that anthroposophy grew out of the general interests of humanity, and to recognize that it had to find access to the Theosophical Society only because that is where the questioners were to be found; that it had to find 'accommodation' there for a while because such 'accommodation' was not to be found anywhere else.

You see, soon after the first period came to an end, the complete inappropriateness of the theosophical movement for Western life became evident, particularly in its approach to the issues surrounding Christ. Where Blavatsky's contempt for Christianity was still basically theoretical, albeit with an emotional basis, the theosophical movement later turned this contempt into practice to the extent that a boy was specially brought up with the intention of making him the vehicle for the resurrection of Christ. There is hardly anything more absurd. An Order[55] was established out of the Theosophical Society with the aim of engineering the birth of Christ in a boy who was actually already here.

This soon descended into total farce. Very soon ambiguities are, of course, introduced in such things that come terribly close to untruths. A congress of the Theosophical Society was to take place in Genoa in 1911.[56] The things leading to such an absurd situation were already well underway and I felt it necessary to announce my lecture 'From Buddha to Christ' for this congress in Genoa. This should have resulted in a clear and concise debate by bringing into the open everything which was already in the air. But—surprise, surprise—the Genoa congress was cancelled. It is, of course, easy to find excuses for something like that, and every word that was uttered sounded uncommonly like an excuse.

Thus we can say that the anthroposophical movement entered its second stage by pursuing its straight course, and it was introduced by a lecture which I delivered to a non-theosophical audience of which only one person—no more!—is still with us, although many people attended the original lecture. But that first lecture I gave, a lecture cycle in fact, was entitled 'From Buddha to Christ'. In 1911 I had wanted to deliver the same cycle again: 'From Buddha to Christ'. There was the straight course! But the theosophical movement had become caught up in a hideous zig-zag course.

If the history of the anthroposophical movement fails to be taken seriously and these things are not properly identified, it is also impossible to give a proper answer to the superficial points which are continually raised about the relationship between anthroposophy and theosophy; points made by people who refuse absolutely to acknowledge that anthroposophy was something quite independent from the beginning, and that it was quite natural for anthroposophy to provide the answers it possessed to the questions which were being asked.

Thus we might say that the second period of the anthroposophical movement lasted until 1914. During that time it did nothing in particular, at least as far as I am concerned, to regulate its relationship with the theosophical movement. The Theosophical Society regulated it when it expelled the anthroposophists.[57] But that was not of any concern. Because from the beginning it was not of any concern to be in the Theosophical Society, it was not of any concern now to be out of it. We simply continued as before. Being excluded changed nothing at all with regard to what happened earlier while we were included.

If you look at how things went, you will see that with the exception of dealing with a few formalities nothing at all was done within the anthroposophical movement until 1914, and that everything which was done was initiated by the Theosophical Society. I was invited at the beginning to give lectures there. That is what I did. I gave anthroposophical lectures. I also continued to do that. I was invited on the basis of those lectures, which have been reprinted in my book *Mystics after Modernism*. I then proceeded to develop in various directions the material contained in *Mystics after Modernism*.

I, and of course my supporters, were then excluded by these same views from the Society. I was included for the same material for which I was later excluded. So that is how it was. The history of the anthroposophical movement will not be understood until the fundamental fact is recognized that it was irrelevant whether I was included in or excluded from the theosophical movement.

That is something which I would ask you to consider thoroughly in your self-reflection. Then, on this basis, I would like to outline tomorrow the last phase, the most difficult one, the one from 1914 until now, and then go on to deal with the details later on in the following lectures.

# LECTURE SIX

## DORNACH, 15 JUNE 1923

I HAVE given you some idea of the forces which determined the first two periods of the anthroposophical movement. But in order to create a basis on which to describe what happened in the third stage, I still wish to deal with a number of phenomena from the first two. It is the case, after all, that despite everything that has been set out, the question can still be raised: What was the reason that the anthroposophical movement nevertheless found itself in a rather external union with the theosophical movement?

This question in particular, which is so complicated, can only be answered if we consider some phenomena which are characteristic of the development of the anthroposophical movement.

So I would like to begin by roughly describing the first period, up until about 1907, as being concerned at the time with developing the fundamentals of the content for a science of the spirit.

Anyone who tries by means of the documents to look back at that time will be able to see that back then the content, the fundamental content of spiritual science in the sense that we have to think of it in terms of anthroposophy, gradually emerged in lectures, lecture cycles and in subsequent work undertaken by others involved. This period concludes—these things are of course only approximately correct, but that's how things are in historical development—with the publication of my *Occult Science*.[58]

*Occult Science* actually only appeared in print some one-and-a-half years later, but the essential content, the publicizing of its essential content undoubtedly falls into this first period of anthroposophical striving. In this period a certain hope was absolutely justified up to

1905 or 1906. It was the hope that the content of anthroposophy might become the purpose of the Theosophical Society's existence.

Until 1905 or 1906 it could not be said that the Theosophical Society would not gradually grow into an anthroposophical one through quite natural development. It was quite possible to hope for this because during these years one of the most important personalities of the Theosophical Society, Annie Besant, displayed a certain tolerance in her outward life, and she certainly strove to allow different directions to work side by side. This was certainly the case until about 1905 and 1906.

During this time it would have been an illusion not to recognize that specifically a leading personality in the Theosophical Society such as Annie Besant had a very primitive understanding of modern scientific method; that is what she had. Nevertheless, despite the amateurish stamp which this gave to all her books, there was a certain sum of wisdom, mostly unprocessed, in the people who belonged to the Society. This became more marked as the focus of the Theosophical Society gradually moved to London and slowly began to feed, in a manner of speaking, on oriental wisdom. This wisdom sometimes led to the most peculiar ideas. But if we ignore the fact that such ideas were sometimes stretched so far that they lost all similarity to their origins and true meaning, something flows through such books as Annie Besant's *Ancient Wisdom*, *The Progress of Mankind*, and even *Christianity* which, although passed down by tradition, originated in ancient sources of wisdom—although the channels through which this ancient wisdom had flowed into those books and lectures were not always flawless. So that was the state of affairs at that time.

On the other hand we must always be aware that in the modern world beyond these circles there was no interest whatsoever in real spiritual research. The reality was simply that the possibility of kindling an interest in a truly modern science of the spirit existed only among those who found their way into this group of people.

Yet within this first period in particular there was a great deal to overcome. I don't even want to bother you with the fact that simply the name 'Theosophy' was adopted by very many societies, societies which basically had very little to do with serious spiritual striving. Many people were working towards something, but it was in part a very egoistic and shallow striving. But even such superficial societies frequently called themselves theosophical. We need only recall, for instance, that quite widely distributed, in Central Europe, in Germany, Austria and also Switzerland, there were certain theosophical branches which possessed only an exceedingly anaemic version of what the Theosophical Society had, in turn saturated with all kinds of sometimes very foolish occult views.

One person who was very active in such societies was someone who is probably familiar to you, or many of you, by name: Franz Hartmann.[59] But the kind of 'profound spirit' and 'deep seriousness', in quotes, which existed in these shallow societies will become obvious to you if I describe the cynical character of this particular leader. He once spoke in a small gathering, at which I was also present—we can certainly have a psychological interest in these things in order to see how the human soul can actually come to this or that. The Theosophical Society was at one time engaged in a dispute in connection with an American called Judge.[60] I don't want to speak about this dispute, but I will only say that the dispute centred on whether certain messages sent out by Judge came from personalities who were higher initiates, so-called Masters. So Franz Hartmann said: Well, that business with Judge, I'm quite familiar with it. He sent out these Mahatma Letters in America. He came to India at the time. We were at the headquarters in India and he wanted the Mahatma Letters so that he would gain authority in America, so that he could say he had been given a mission by initiates. So I told him, Franz Hartmann recounted, Mahatma Letters? I can write some for you. So Judge responded: But that won't work, then I can't claim that they are Mahatma Letters because they are supposed to fly towards you through the air; they originate in a magical way and then land on your head, and that is what I have to be able to say. So Hartmann said to Judge—he recounted this himself!—Oh, don't worry, that can be done. Judge was a very small fellow, Hartmann told us, and so he said to him: Stand on the floor and I will stand on a chair and then I will drop the letter on your head. Then Judge could say with a clear conscience that he was distributing letters which had landed on his head out of the air.

That is an extreme example of things which are not at all rare in the world. But as I said, I do not really want to waste your time with these shallow societies. I only want to point out that the close proximity of the anthroposophical to the theosophical movement made it necessary for the former to defend itself against modern scientific thinking during its first period.

I do not know whether those who subsequently joined the anthroposophical movement—and as scientists and from a scientific perspective observed anthroposophy, which was by then more developed, during its third stage—have gained sufficient insight into the fact that a critical assessment of modern scientific thinking took place in a very specific way during the first period of the anthroposophical movement. I only give examples because this process occurred in a number of different areas. But these examples will show you how the theosophical movement was strongly influenced by what I described here a few days ago as particularly characteristic of modern education: the way it bows down to so-called scientific authority.

Such bowing down to scientific authority had penetrated the Theosophical Society in particular. It turned out that Annie Besant, for instance, tried to use in her books all kinds of quotes from contemporary science, such as Weismann's theory of heredity,[61] which bore no relevance to the science of the spirit. She used them as if they provided some sort of evidence. Now if you recall, at the time when we were in a position to start a kind of centre for the anthroposophical movement in Munich—gradually, the Berlin, the Munich, the Stuttgart, the Kassel, the Düsseldorf, the Cologne, the Hamburg, the Hanover, the Leipzig centres were developing; in Austria the Vienna one, in a certain sense even the one in Prague; in other words, centres were developing—there were many such homeless souls there which were also already organized in a certain sense. They were in one or the other society. Now I want to disregard completely the shallow societies of Hartmann's kind but I want to mention that while we were establishing the branch in Munich it became necessary to assess critically the various larger and smaller groups which were then in existence.

There was one group called the Ketterl. This Ketterl consisted of extremely scholarly people. In the Ketterl these people were very much concerned with providing proofs from natural science for the claims which were made on behalf of spiritual science. Their concern was to rise from the views that were prevalent in natural science to those which anthroposophy, for example, represented. When anthroposophy spoke about the etheric body, they would say that science has recognized this or that structure for atoms and molecules. Then they began to investigate how such structures could become partly more complicated, partly thinner in their composition, in order to gradually move from the molecular structure of the physical bodies to the molecular structure of the ether. It would then be possible to make the kind of calculations for etheric events as can be done for physical events. And actually only those things which had a legally valid scientific visa on their anthroposophical passport were to be admitted in the Ketterl.

The papers—for such papers do indeed exist—which the members of the Ketterl wrote were not really very different from the scientific papers of the theoretical physicists of the time; the formulae and definitions and so on were applied not to processes of the spectrum or in the electromagnetic field but to processes in the etheric or astral field. There was nothing to be done. The whole thing dissolved more or less amicably. In the end we no longer had any links with these investigators from the scientific point of view.

Not so very different from these Ketterl studies were the efforts of a man who played a major role in the Theosophical Society, a close friend still of Blavatsky, an omnipresent man when it came to such matters, Dr Hübbe-Schleiden,[62] who edited *Sphinx* for a long time. He, too, was obsessed with proving what he felt was theosophical subject matter by means of natural scientific thinking. I remember how he met me at the station in Hanover the first time because I was due to give a lecture, the first anthroposophical lecture I gave in Hanover: an examination of Goethe's *Fairy Tale of the Green Snake and the Beautiful Lily*. He took me to his home, a little way outside

Hanover. It was perhaps half an hour by tram. He immediately began to explain with tremendous enthusiasm how such things as spiritual findings could not endure among modern people if things were not proven in the way that people were used to seeing in physics or other contemporary textbooks. He then spent the entire half-hour describing with the tips of his index fingers the motion which was meant to show how atoms move: Yes, it has to happen in this way and that way and then we have the answer. The atoms move in one incarnation, and then the wave packet continues through the spiritual worlds and now it has to be calculated how the wave packet passes through the spiritual worlds. Then this changes and that is the next incarnation. So it really felt like you were back in the lecture hall in which you used to be taught the wave packets for red and yellow and blue and green. The wave packets for the passage of souls through the various incarnations were entirely of the same nature. In the same way as the Newtonians, and modern physicists in general, calculate light in terms of wave packets, so he calculated the passage of souls through various incarnations.

He had a friend, who then became an extraordinarily good, understanding and loyal member of the Anthroposophical Society, to whom he always sent his studies. One of the qualities of this friend was that he thought very highly of these studies; but his sense of humour kept getting the better of him, and on one occasion he told me that he had been sent another thirty kilos of wisdom to Munich by Dr Hübbe-Schleiden. Because the letters that kept being sent from Hanover to Munich were so bulky.

Now let me say that a special version of this way of thinking was evident in the debate about the 'permanent atom' which took place in the Theosophical Society over a long period. This 'permanent atom' was something awful, but was taken incredibly seriously. For, you see, the people who felt the full weight of modern science could not understand why something which at least had the terminology of modern science shouldn't penetrate spiritual science. So they said: Well, a person lives in one incarnation and then in the next. True, the physical body decomposes, only a single atom remains, which then passes through the time between death and a new birth. And this atom appears in the new incarnation. This is the permanent atom which passes through incarnations.

This may appear funny to you today, but you simply cannot understand the seriousness with which these things were pursued, specifically in the first period of the anthroposophical cause, and the difficulty which existed in responding to the challenge: What, indeed, is the point of theosophy if it cannot be proved scientifically! No one will accept it if it cannot be proved scientifically. During that conversation in the tram the point was undeniably made that things have to be presented in a manner which will allow a graduated schoolboy to understand theosophy in the same way that he understands logic. That was the thrust of my companion's argument.

Then we arrived at his home and he took me into the loft. Now I would ask those who now in the last period of the anthroposophical movement are striving to fight against atomism to consider what I found at that time in the loft of Dr Hübbe-Schleiden in Hanover. So we went up a narrow flight of stairs, and up there— in telling this, I have to repeat that he was an exceedingly kind, pleasant and intelligent man; in other words, a sympathetic old gentleman—up there in the loft were giant models of atoms. They were made of wire, very complex. One of the models always represented the atom of some physical body: hydrogen or oxygen; the next model, which was even more complex, would represent the atom of something etheric; the third model, still more complex, was an atom of something astral.

If you pick up certain books by a leading figure in the Theosophical Society, Leadbeater's books,[63] you will find such models drawn in extravagant form. I would also still like to mention the fact, for those to consider who today are fighting against atomism in our midst, that such atomism flourished nowhere as greatly as among those who joined our ranks from the Theosophical Society. And when younger members such as Dr Kolisko[64] and the others at our research institute in Stuttgart[65] are engaged in the fight against the atom, we might well recall that certain people at that time would not have known how to get from one incarnation to the next without at least one permanent atom.

That is something of an image of the way in which the strong
authority of so-called natural scientific thinking exerted its influence
in these circles. These people could undoubtedly think in natural
scientific terms. They were unable to conceive of any other valid
way of thinking than the natural scientific one. So there was no real
understanding in this quarter either. Only as the anthroposophical
movement entered its second stage did these atomistic endeavours
gradually subside, at least within those circles who joined our ranks,
and there was a gradual transition to the subject matter which continued to be cultivated in the anthroposophical movement. But on
the other hand it must be said that those who did not care much for
this atomic striving, who were quite indifferent to modern science,
who were inspired by the theosophical movement only because they
were homeless souls, were always more amenable. Every time I was
in Munich, for instance, it was possible to give a lecture designed
more for the group which gathered round the former great friend of
Blavatsky's, Mrs von Schewitsch.[66] Things were easier there because
a genuine inner striving existed.

I neither want to defend the one group nor criticize the other,
but only want to mention how the anthroposophical movement
handled these things in one direction or the other. But just think,
within our own ranks, too, there was a call at that time to justify
the content of anthroposophy using the current natural scientific
way of thinking. It was less radical, nevertheless, than the demands
made by external critics today. A large number of you heard Dr
Blümel's[67] lecture today—I'm sure you will have understood
his illuminating account very well and will have received a certain impression. But imagine if someone had sat there who said:
Everything explained there is not of my concern. I don't believe
it; I don't accept anything; I don't want to test it. Someone else
might say: See whether it is accurate, examine it with your reason
and your soul faculties. I don't want to, says the first person; it is
no business of mine be it right or wrong; I do not want to become
involved with that. But I call on Dr Blümel to go to a psychological laboratory and there, using my psychological methods, I will
examine whether or not he is a mathematician.

That is, of course, piffle of the first order. But it is exactly the demand made today by the outside world that the anthroposophical researcher should go to a psychological laboratory in order to determine there whether they have the right to make their claims or analyses. It is exactly the same.

Sadly, it is quite possible today to talk nonsense, pure nonsense and people don't notice it. Even those who are upset by it fail to notice that it is pure nonsense. They believe that it is only maliciousness or something similar, because they cannot imagine that social circumstances could somehow lead someone to become an official representative of science while actually talking pure nonsense. That is the extent to which our spiritual life has become confused.

So the things that have to be taken into account when talking about the conditions under which the anthroposophical movement can exist have to be sought wholly in the cultural phenomena and cultural impulses of the present. The kind of things which I am explaining here must be understood by anyone who wants to grasp the position of the anthroposophical movement.

Well, undeterred by all that, the most important human truths, the most important cosmic truths, had to be made public during the first stage. My *Occult Science* represents a sort of compendium of everything which had been put forward in the anthroposophical movement until that point. It worked in the way it did only for the reason that our intention was always a concrete and never an abstract one, because we never attempted to do more than could be achieved in the given circumstances.

Let me quote the following as evidence. We established a journal, *Luzifer-Gnosis*,[68] right at the outset of the anthroposophical movement. At first it was called *Luzifer*. Then, when five or six issues had appeared, a Viennese journal called *Gnosis* wanted to amalgamate with it. Let me mention in passing in this connection that I simply wanted to express the outer union between these two journals by intending to give the new journal the title Luzifer with Gnosis. Of course that was completely unacceptable to Hübbe-Schleiden, for instance, who thought that this would indicate an unnatural union, Luzifer with Gnosis. Well, I was not particularly bothered, so we called it *Luzifer-Gnosis* with a hyphen. People were very sharp-witted and they were keeping a close eye on us at that time!

So the journal *Luzifer-Gnosis* was founded. Of course we started with a very small number of subscribers, but it began to grow at a very fast pace, relatively speaking, and we never really ran at a deficit because we only ever printed approximately as many copies as we were able to sell. The mechanics of it went like this, that once an issue had been written and printed, the copies were sent to my house in large parcels. Then my wife and I put the wrappers around them. I addressed them myself and then each of us took a washing basket and carried the whole lot to the post office. We found that this worked quite well. I wrote and held lectures while my wife organized the whole Anthroposophical Society,[69] but without a secretary, because if she had had a secretary, she would have been working for them as well. So we did that all on our own and never attempted more than could be managed on a practical level. We did not even, for example, take larger washing baskets than we could manage—just. When the number of subscribers grew we simply made an extra journey.

Then, when we had been engaged in this interesting activity for some time, *Luzifer-Gnosis* passed to the publisher Altmann in Leipzig. And then it ceased publication—not because it had to, for it had many more subscribers than it needed at the time, but because I no longer had the time to write.

It was indeed the case that then the demands of my lecturing activity and of the spiritual administration of the Society in general began to take up a lot of time—the whole thing was a very slow and gradual process—leading to *Luzifer-Gnosis* no longer appearing. At first there were long gaps, the January issue appeared in December, and then one year turned into a year-and-a-half, and the subscribers made a terrible fuss. Altmann, the publisher, received a whole lot of complaints, so that I had no alternative but to tell him: Well, we'll just have to stop altogether and tell the subscribers that no matter how long they wait, there won't be any more!

Well, this of course also reflected the inner course of develop-ment: we never wanted more than could be managed at each practi-cal step. This belongs to the conditions which govern the existence of a spiritual society. To build far-reaching ideals on phrases is the worst thing which can happen to a spiritual society; setting up programmes is the worst thing which can happen to a spiritual society. The work in this first period was such that to begin with in 1907, 1908, 1909 the foundations of a science of the spirit appropriate to the modern age were put in place.

Then came the second phase, which was essentially concluded when we had come to grips with natural science. The theologians had not yet made their presence felt. They were still seated so firmly in the saddle everywhere that they were simply not bothered.

When the analysis of the natural sciences was finished, we were able to approach our other task. This was the analysis of the Gospels, Genesis, the Christian tradition as a whole, Christianity as such.

The thread had already been laid out in my book *Christianity As Mystical Fact* which stood at the starting point. It appeared as early as 1902. But the elaboration, as it were, of an anthroposophical understanding of Christianity was essentially the task of the second stage up to approximately 1914. As a consequence I gave lecture cycles on the various parts of the Christian tradition in Hamburg, Kassel, Berlin, Basle, Berne, Munich and Stuttgart.

That was also when, for instance, *The Spiritual Guidance of the Individual and Humanity*[70] was worked out, which until then had only existed in outline. It was, then, essentially the time in which the Christian side of anthroposophy was worked out, following on from the historical tradition of Christianity.

This period also included what I might call the first expansion of anthroposophy into the artistic field, with performances of the Mystery Dramas in Munich.[71] That, too, took place against the background of never wanting to achieve more than circumstances allowed.

Also during this time those events occurred which led to the exclusion from the Theosophical Society, a fact which was actually of no great significance for anthroposophy, given that, as I said yesterday evening, it was irrelevant to anthroposophy whether it was included or excluded since it had followed its own path from the beginning. Those who wanted to come along were free to do so. From the outset anthroposophy did not concern itself inwardly with the spiritual content which came from the Theosophical Society. But outer coexistence became increasingly difficult as well.

At the beginning there was a definite hope that circumstances, some of which at least I have described, might allow the theosophical movement which had come together in the Theosophical Society to become truly anthroposophical. The circumstances which made such a hope appear justified included the serious disappointment about the particular methods of investigation pursued by the Theosophical Society, specifically among those people who possessed a higher level of discrimination. And I have to say that when I arrived in London on both the first and second visits, I experienced how its leaders were basically people who adopted a very sceptical attitude towards one another, who felt themselves to be on very insecure ground which, however, they did not want to leave because they did not know where to look for security.

There were many disappointed people who had great reservations, particularly among the leaders of the Theosophical Society. The peculiar change which took place in Annie Besant from 1900 to, say, 1907 is an important factor in the subsequent course of events in the Theosophical Society.

She possessed a certain tolerance to begin with. I believe she never really understood the phenomenon of anthroposophy, but she accepted it and at the beginning even defended it, that is its right to exist, against the rigid dogmatists. That is how we must describe it, for that is how it was.

But there is something I must say which I would also urge members of the Anthroposophical Society to consider very seriously. Certain personal aspirations, purely personal sympathies and antipathies, are absolutely irreconcilable with a spiritual society of this kind, including of the kind the theosophical was. Nevertheless, there are so many cases in particular where someone actually wants this or that. Someone, for instance, begins to idolize someone else, for whatever underlying reasons within themselves. They will not acknowledge whatever compulsion it is, and sometimes it can be an intellectual compulsion that drives them to do it. But they begin to

weave an artificial astral aura around the individual whom they want
to idolize. The latter then becomes advanced. If they want to make
an especially telling remark they will say: Oh, that individual is aware
of three or four previous lives on earth and even spoke to me about
my earlier earth lives. That person knows a lot! And this is precisely
what leads to a spiritual interpretation of something which is human,
all too human, to use an expression of Nietzsche's.

If someone were to say: I idolize that person—that might be a bit
excessive, but they could say: I like that person, I will not deny that I
like them. Then everything would be fine, even in esoteric societies.
Max Seiling,[72] for instance, was very amusing in certain ways, particularly when he played the piano in that effervescent way of his, and
he was amusing to have tea with and so on. All would have been well
if people had admitted it. If people had admitted: We like that. That
would have been more sensible than idolizing him in the way the
Munich group did.

You see, all these things are in direct contradiction to the conditions under which such a society should exist. And the prime example of someone who fell prey to this kind of thing is Annie Besant.
For example—and I prefer to speak about these things by quoting
facts—a name cropped up on one occasion. I did not bother much
with the literature produced by the Theosophical Society, basically
I read very little of that literature, and so I became acquainted with
the name Bhagavân Dâs[73] only when a thick typewritten manuscript
arrived one day. The manuscript was arranged in two columns, with
text on the left side and a blank on the right. Attached was a letter
from Bhagavân Dâs, this was in about 1905 I think, which said that
he wanted to discuss with various people the subject matter which he
intended to reveal to the world through the manuscript.

Well, the anthroposophical movement was already so widespread
at that time that I did not manage to read the manuscript immediately. He said one should write what one had to add on the right-
hand side and then send it back to him.

I got around a bit at the time. I also found other people to whom
he had sent the manuscript. Then I increasingly realized: Bhagavân Dâs was, well, a 'very esoteric person', a person who drew his

inspiration from profound spiritual sources. That was approximately the view which people associated with Annie Besant spread about Bhagavân Dâs. Since he sent the thing from India, had a close connection to the Indian headquarters and had acquired some fame—for example, at the Amsterdam congress[74] the name Bhagavân Dâs was on everyone's lips—it was really as if there were a fountain here that was constantly overflowing with wisdom. So I decided to have a look at the thing: a horrendously amateurish confusion of Fichtean philosophy, Hegelian philosophy, and Schopenhauer's philosophy; everything mixed up together without the slightest understanding. And the whole thing was held together by 'self' and 'not self', like an endlessly repeated tune. Then something about Fichte again and so on, and then again 'self' and 'not self'. It was excruciating. I never bothered with it again. I didn't write anything on the other side. But as you can see, something like this shows how things can gradually get personal. The idolization of Bhagavân Dâs was based purely on personal considerations. You can still read his books today and you will find what I said to be true. It is the case that he concocted such books. Such things demonstrate how the personal element is introduced into impulses which should be objective. The first step on the slippery slope was taken with the appearance of this phenomenon, which became increasingly strong from about 1905 onwards. Everything else was basically a consequence of that.

I do not mean to say by this that in any given society, if someone writes nonsense, that society must crash. But different laws, inner necessities prevail in spiritual societies. Here such things must not be practised by their leading personalities, otherwise they will, of necessity, slide down the slippery slope. That is, indeed, what happened.

Then there was the absurd tale connected with Olcott's death,[75] which occurred at that time, and which was actually already the beginning of the end of the Theosophical Society: the so-called nomination by the Masters. That could at least still be smoothed over by saying that such foolishness was introduced into the Society by particular people, even if they were acting on the basis of certain principles. It was, however, followed by the Leadbeater affair,[76] the details of which I do not want to discuss just now. And then came the discovery of the boy who was to be brought up as Christ, or to become Christ, and so on. And when people who did not want to be involved in these absurd matters refused to accept them, they were simply expelled.

Well, the anthroposophical movement followed its straight course throughout the whole of this business and as a movement basically did not bother with these things. You see, if say in 1911 you were doing research on 'The Spiritual Guidance of the Individual and Humanity' on 24 March, and on 25 March the absurd reports from the Theosophical Society arrived from Adyar or elsewhere, that did not mean that on 25 March you had to continue what you had been doing on the 24th in any other way. The inner course was really not affected at all. That has to be made absolutely clear. It really was a matter of supreme indifference at the time what came from various sides from the leading personalities of the Theosophical Society— just as I was not especially surprised to hear recently that Leadbeater has become an old Catholic bishop in his old age, and one of his comrades, who was already at the Munich congress, has even become an archbishop. There really is no need to be surprised about these things. There was no sense of direction and everything was going topsy turvy. Why shouldn't something like that happen either?

Indeed, there was no particular need for a person to change their personal relationship with these people, I mean the direct day-to-day relationship. Two years ago I think it was, I gave a lecture in Amsterdam.[77] After the lecture, one of the gentleman who had delivered a lecture at the Munich congress in 1907[78] approached me with the old cordial spirit. He still looked the same, but in the meantime he had become an old Catholic archbishop. He was not wearing the garments, but that is what he was!

These are all things that simply took place in an arena of modern cultural life in which, on the other hand, it truly was the case that the homeless souls were attracted out of an inner necessity. It must not be forgotten that in the stream we have been describing could also be found precisely those souls who were searching most intensively for a link between the human soul and the spiritual world. We are not being honest about the course of modern culture if these contrasts are not on occasion made absolutely clear. That is why I had to make these additional points today, my dear friends, before going on tomorrow to describe the last phase, and thus the actual conditions which underlie the existence of the Anthroposophical Society.

# LECTURE SEVEN

## DORNACH, 16 JUNE 1923

Having talked about various outer circumstances as well as the more intimate aspects of modern spiritual movements, which should in a sense find a path which really corresponds to the demands of our time through the anthroposophical movement, I will attempt today and tomorrow to provide an interpretation of the conditions which govern the existence of the Anthroposophical Society in particular. And I will do so by means of various events which have occurred during the third phase of the anthroposophical movement.

We have to understand clearly our position at the time when the second phase of the anthroposophical movement was coming to an end, around 1913 and 1914, and our position today. We must try to penetrate what the two stages, I would say, at the beginning of the third period and at the end of the third period mean for us.

While in the past few days I have tried to a greater extent to go into the depths in my account, today and tomorrow I would like to present to a greater extent topics which are, in a manner of speaking, of current relevance for anthroposophists and which are suitable to pass directly into the will impulses.

Let us look back at the progress which was achieved in the first and second phases by adhering essentially to the principle that progress should be made in line with actual circumstances, that the movement should move forward at the same speed as the inner life of anthroposophy expands, at how far that took us. Let us look at that.

I said that in the first phase—approximately up to 1907, 1908, 1909—we gradually worked out the inner spiritual content. The foundations were laid for a truly modern science of the spirit with the consequences which that entailed in various directions. The journal *Luzifer-Gnosis* was produced until the end of that period. It regularly carried material by me and others which built up the content of anthroposophy in stages. When the second phase began, spiritual research came to grips in lectures and lecture cycles with those texts which are particularly significant for the spiritual development of the West, the Gospels and Genesis, a development which included the broader public in certain ways. Once again real progress was made.

We started with the Gospel of St John, and moved from there to the other Gospels. They were used to demonstrate certain wisdom and truths. The spiritual content was built up with each step. The expansion of the Society was essentially linked with this inner development of its spiritual content.

Of course programmes and similar things had to be organized to take care of everyday business. But that was not the priority. The main thing was that positive spiritual work was undertaken at each stage and that these spiritual achievements could then be deepened esoterically in the appropriate way.

In this context it was particularly at the end of the second phase that anthroposophy spread more widely into general culture and civilization, as with the Munich performances of the Mystery Dramas. We reached the stage at the end of the second phase when we could begin to think about the construction of the building which has suffered such a misfortune here. We have to remember that this was an exceedingly important stage in the development of the Anthroposophical Society. The construction of such a building assumed that a considerable number of people had an interest in creating a home for the real substance of anthroposophy. But it also meant that the first significant step was being taken beyond the measured progress which had kept pace with the overall development of the Anthroposophical Society. Because it is obvious that a building like the Goetheanum, in contrast to everything that had gone before, would focus the attention of the world at large in quite a different way on what the Society had become.

We had our opponents previously, opponents in various camps. They even went so far as to publish what they said about us. But they failed to draw people's attention. It was the construction of the building which first created the opportunity for our opponents to find an audience. For suppose for a moment that up to 1914 such an unqualified opponent as Max Seiling had appeared. Perhaps some members of the Anthroposophical Society might have read it [what he wrote] themselves out of a certain sensational interest, but no one outside would have cared. There would have been no audience for it. The construction of the building made it possible for opponents to appear and find an audience. When we have the reality of something such as the anthroposophical movement, such things must not be regarded merely as something to be considered theoretically, but must be taken most seriously, for greater tasks arise from all these things day by day.

We nevertheless had the opportunity to construct this building. This opportunity assumed that something existed which made it worthwhile to do that. It did exist. A larger number of people experienced its presence as something with a certain inner vitality. Indeed, we had gathered valuable experience over a considerable period of time. Since a Society existed, this experience could have been put to good use, could be put to good use today. Everything I have spoken about in the last few days was meant to point to certain events which can be taken as valuable experience.

Now this period has come to an end. The fire at the Goetheanum represents the shattering event which demonstrated that this period has come to an end. Remember that I said that these lectures are also intended to allow for self-reflection among anthroposophists. That self-reflection should lead us to remember today how we could think about the progress of what was intended with anthroposophy with a kind of certainty but how at that time we also had to anticipate, anticipate actively, that when anthroposophy stepped into the limelight the opposition would inevitably grow.

Now we are talking in the first instance about the start and the finish. The start I have just characterized. It is represented in the courage to begin the construction of the Goetheanum. Let us examine in what form the effect achieved by the Goetheanum, in that it exposed anthroposophy to the judgement of an unlimited number of people, is evident today.

To that end I want to show you the latest evidence, so that we stay with the topic, as it were. The latest evidence is contained in a pamphlet which has just appeared and which is entitled *The Secret Machinery of Revolution*.[79] On page 13 of this pamphlet you will find the following exposition. I will translate it from the English:

> At this stage of my inquiry I may refer briefly to the existence of an offshoot of the Theosophical Society, known as the Anthroposophical Society. This was formed as the result of a schism in the ranks of the Theosophists, by a man of Jewish birth who was connected with one of the modern branches of the Carbonari. Not only so, but in association with another Theosophist he is engaged in organizing certain singular commercial undertakings not unconnected with Communist propaganda; almost precisely in the manner in which Count St. Germain[80] organized his dyeworks and other commercial ventures with a like purpose. And this queer business group has its connections with the Irish Republican movement, with the German groups already mentioned the groups mentioned includes for example the organization Consul, and also with another mysterious group, known as Clarté, which was founded by Jewish intellectuals in France about four years ago, and which includes in its membership many well-known politicians, scientists, university professors, and literary men in France, Germany and England. It is a secret society, but some idea of its real aims may be gathered from the fact that it sponsored the Ligue des Anciens Combatants, whose aim appears to be to undermine the discipline of the armies in the Allied countries. Although nominally a Right Wing society, it is in direct touch with members of the Soviet Government of Russia; in Britain it is also connected with certain Fabians and with the Union of Democratic Control, which opposes secret diplomacy.

The only thing I need add is that my trip to London is planned for August, and you can see from this that the things I have often said should be taken very seriously: that our opponents are very well organized and know very well in every situation what they are doing. As you know, I have said for some time that one should never believe there is not always a worse surprise in store.

As you can see, we have our opponents today—and that is the other point which marks the end of the third phase—who are not afraid to make use of any lie and who know very well how to utilize it to best advantage. It is wrong to believe that it is somehow appropriate to pass over these things lightly with the argument that not only are they devoid of truth, but the lies are so crude no one will believe them. People who say that, my dear friends, simply show that they are deeply unaware of the nature of contemporary Western culture, and do not recognize the powerful impulses to untruth which, I have to say, are accepted as true even by the best people, because it is convenient and they are only half awake.

For us it is particularly important to look at what lies between these two points. Because it would be true to say that in 1914 the anthroposophical movement had undoubtedly reached the point at which it could have survived in the world on the strength of its own spiritual resources, its spiritual content.

But conditions dictated that we should continue to work with vitality after 1914. If we look back at what has happened since that time, we can say that the work since then consisted essentially of a spiritual deepening. And in that respect we took the direct path once again. We sought that spiritual deepening stage by stage, without concern for the external events of the world, because it was and still is the case that the spiritual content which needs to be revealed for humanity to progress has to be incorporated into our civilization initially in any form available. We can never do anything in speaking about or working on this spiritual material other than base our actions on this spiritual material itself.

In this respect anthroposophy was broadened in its third phase through the introduction of eurythmy. No one can ever claim that eurythmy is based on anything other than the sources of anthroposophy. Everything is taken from the sources of anthroposophy. After all, there are at present all kinds of dance forms which attempt in one way or another to achieve something which might superficially resemble eurythmy to a certain extent. But look at events from the point when Marie Steiner took charge of eurythmy,[81] so that during the War it was cultivated in what I might describe as internal circles, but then it became public and met with ever increasing interest. Look at everything which has contributed to eurythmy. Believe me, there were many people who insinuated that here or there something very similar existed which had to be taken into account or incorporated into eurythmy. The only way in which fruitful progress could be made was to look neither to left nor right but simply work directly from the sources themselves, only from the sources themselves. If any compromise had been introduced, eurythmy would no longer be what it is, would not have been able to turn into what it has become. That is one of the conditions which govern the existence of such a movement; there must be an absolute certainty that the material required can be gathered directly from the sources in a continuous process of expansion.

Working from the centre like this, which was, of course, relatively easy until 1914 because it was self-evident, is the only way to make proper progress with anthroposophy.

This third period, from 1914 onwards, witnessed the most all-encompassing phenomenon which naturally affected the anthroposophical movement as it affected everything else. Now it must be strongly emphasized, on the one hand, that during the War, when countries were tearing each other apart, members of sixteen or seventeen nations were present here and working together; it must be emphasized that the Anthroposophical Society passed through this period without in any way forfeiting its essential nature. But neither must it be forgotten that all the feelings which passed through people's minds during this period, and thus also through the minds of anthroposophists, had a splintering effect on the Anthroposophical Society in many respects. This cannot be denied.

In truth, in talking about these things in an objective manner, I do not want to criticize or invalidate in any way the good characteristics which anthroposophists possess. We should take them for granted. It is true that within the Anthroposophical Society we managed to overcome to a certain extent the things which so divided people between 1914 and 1918. But anyone watching these things a little will have noticed that the Society could not avoid the ripple effect, even if it appeared in a somewhat different form from usual, and that in this context something came strongly to the surface which I have described before by saying that in this third phase we saw the beginnings of what I might call a certain inner opposition to the tasks I had to fulfil in the Anthroposophical Society.

Of course most people are surprised when I talk of this inner opposition because they are unaware of it, at least many of them. But I have to say that this does not make it any better, because these feelings of inner opposition grew particularly strongly in the third phase. That was also evident in outer symptoms. When a movement like ours has passed through two phases in the way I have described, there is certainly no need for blind trust when certain actions are taken in the third phase in a context whose full ramifications are not immediately clear to everyone, given that the precedents already exist, that there are preceding events. But remember that these actions were undertaken in a context in which, while most certainly not everyone understood their full implications, many things had to be held together and it was of paramount importance that the anthroposophical movement itself should be defined in the right way. That is when we observed what might be described as such inner opposition.

I am aware, of course, that when I speak about these things, many people will say: But shouldn't we have our own opinions? We should certainly have our own opinions about what we do, but when someone else does something with which one is connected in life it is also true that trust must play some role, particularly when such precedents exist as I have described.

Now at a certain point of the third phase during the War, I wrote the booklet *Thoughts during the Time of War*.[82] This particular work elicited inner opposition which was especially noticeable. Not just that people told me that they thought anthroposophy never intervened in politics—as if that booklet involved itself with politics!—and more such. It was quite possible to see in their whole position that something had affected them in their heart which should not grow on the ground of anthroposophy although it sprouts in quite different soil. So you see, I experienced quite a few such objections to *Thoughts during the Time of War*, but I never experienced, truly never experienced someone saying—I am about to say something terribly arrogant, but objective nevertheless, my dear friends: We can't really make head nor tail of the matter but let's wait until 1935, then we might understand why that booklet was written.

And this is only one example among many which demonstrates clearly the strong intervention of something whose almost exclusive purpose was to undermine the freedom and self-determination within the Anthroposophical Society which we take for granted. It should have been self-evident that the writing of this publication was my business alone. Instead, an opinion began to form: If he wants to be the one with whom we build the Anthroposophical Society, then he is allowed to write only the things we approve of.

These things have to be stated in a direct manner, otherwise they will not be understood. They are symptomatic and they show that a mood arose which ran counter to the conditions governing the existence of the anthroposophical movement, that a mood arose in the Society which ran counter to the conditions governing the existence of the anthroposophical movement!

But what has to play a particularly significant role in this third phase is the awareness of having created a Society which has taken the first steps along a road which a large part of humanity will later follow. Just consider this, my dear friends, that a relatively small Society formed which took upon itself the task of doing something which a large part of humanity is supposed to follow. That creates not only the obligations which will then be incumbent on those who come later, but that creates obligations of a far higher kind: that creates obligations which are many times greater than those which will one day be the obligations of a large number of people who will take anthroposophy as their orientation.

Anthroposophists today must not think that they have only the same commitments which future anthroposophists will have when they exist by the million rather than the thousand. When thousands are active in the vanguard of a movement, these thousands have to show commitment of an exponentially higher order. It means that they are obliged to show greater courage, greater energy, greater patience, greater tolerance and, above all, greater truthfulness in every respect. And in this third stage specifically the test was set with regard to our truthfulness and seriousness. It related in a certain sense to the subject matter discussed at one point in the lectures to theologians.[83] That is where it was raised. Irrespective of the fact that there are individual anthroposophists, a feeling should have developed—must develop!—among them that Anthroposophia exists as a separate being who moves about among us, as it were; towards whom we carry a responsibility in every moment of our lives. That is what was expressed in those lectures to the theologians: Anthroposophia is actually an invisible person who walks among visible people and towards whom we must show the greatest responsibility for as long as we are a small group. Anthroposophia is someone who must be understood as an invisible person, as someone with a real existence, who should be consulted in the individual actions of our lives.

Thus, if connections form between people—friendships, cliques and so on—at a time when the group of anthroposophists is still small, it is all the more necessary to consult and to be able to justify all our actions before this invisible person.

This will, of course, apply less and less as anthroposophy spreads. But as long as it remains the property of a small group of people, it is necessary for every action to follow from consultation with the person Anthroposophia. That anthroposophy should be seen as a living being is an essential condition of its existence. It will only be allowed to die when its group of supporters has expanded immeasurably. What we require, then, is a deeply serious commitment to the invisible person I have just spoken about. That commitment has to grow with every passing day. If this deep commitment does so, there can be no doubt that everything we do will begin and proceed in the right way.

Let me emphasize one fact. While the second phase from 1907, 1908, 1909 to 1914 was essentially a period in which the feeling side, the religious knowledge of anthroposophy, was developed, something recurred in the third phase which was already present in the first, as I described yesterday. It happened that a relationship was again established between anthroposophy and the sciences, for example, the different branches of science.

It was already evident during the War that a number of scientists from various quarters were beginning to lean towards anthroposophy. This meant that the Anthroposophical Society gained collaborators in the scientific field. At first they remained rather in the background. Until 1919 or 1920 the scientific work of the Society remained a hope rather than a reality, with the exception of the fruitful results which Dr Unger[84] achieved on the basis of *The Philosophy of Freedom* and other writings from the pre-anthroposophical period. Otherwise, if we disregard the constructive epistemological work that continued to be done in this respect, which provided an important and substantive basis for the future content of the movement, we have to say that at the start of the third period the scientific aspect remained a hope. For scientific work became effective at this stage in a way exactly opposite to what had happened in the first phase. In the latter period people were concerned, as I explained yesterday, to justify anthroposophy to science; anthroposophy was to have its credentials checked by science. That was the tendency in the first period. Since it was unable to do that, its scientific work slowly dried up. In the second phase it did not exist at all, and towards the end things concentrated more on the artistic side. Universal human interests took the upper hand.

Scientific aspirations emerged again from various quarters in the third phase, but this time in the opposite way. Now they were no longer concerned, at least not primarily, with justifying anthroposophy to science, but rather sought to use anthroposophy to fertilize it. Now all kinds of people came who said that they had reached the limits of their scientific work and were looking for something to fertilize their endeavours. Now it was no longer a case, as it had been in the first period, of inventing atomic structures because people were so used to looking for atomic theories for the etheric and astral bodies on the basis of physics and astronomy. Now, when enough progress had been made to make a contribution to science, the exact opposite occurred.

This tendency—and I wish to discuss only its positive aspects today—will only be effective for the benefit of the anthroposophical movement if it can find a way of working purely from anthroposophical sources, rather in the way that, say, eurythmy has done in the artistic field, and if it is accompanied by the commitment which I have mentioned. As long as so much of the present scientific mode of thinking is carried unconsciously into the anthroposophical movement it will not be able to make progress productively.

In particular, there will be a lack of progress as long as people believe that the current scientific establishment can be persuaded about anything without it first adopting a more positive attitude towards anthroposophy. Once it has done that, a dialogue can begin. Our task with regard to those who are fighting against anthroposophy today can only be to demonstrate clearly where they are not telling the truth. That is something which can be discussed. But of course there can be no dialogue about meritorious[85] matters, matters of content, with people who not only do not want to be convinced, but who cannot be convinced because they lack the necessary basic knowledge.

That, above all, is where the work needs to be done: to create the foundations for ourselves in the various fields, but to do that from the core of anthroposophy, from the central sources.

When an attempt was made after the War to tackle practical issues in people's lives and the problems facing the world, that again had to be done on the basis of anthroposophy, and with the recognition that with these practical tasks in particular it was hardly possible to count on any sort of compromise. The only proper course we can pursue is to tell the world what we have found through anthroposophy itself, and then wait and see how many people are able to understand it. We certainly cannot approach the world with the core material of anthroposophy in the hope that there might be a party or a person who can be won over. That is impossible. That doesn't exist. That is contrary to the fundamental circumstances governing the existence of the anthroposophical movement. Take a women's movement or a social movement, for instance, where it is possible to take the view that we should join and compromise our position because its members' views may incline towards anthroposophy in one way or another; that is absolutely impossible. What matters is to have enough inner security regarding anthroposophy to be able to advocate it under any circumstances.

Let me give you an amusing example of this. Whenever people are angry with me for having used the Theosophical Society for my work, I always reply that I will advocate anthroposophy wherever there is a demand, no matter where. I have done it in places where it was only possible once, for the simple reason that people did not want to hear anything further from me a second time. But I never spoke in a way that, given their inner constitution, they could have been persuaded by superficial charm to listen to me a second time. That is something which has to be avoided. When people demand to hear something we have to present them with anthroposophy, pure anthroposophy, which is drawn with courage from its innermost core.

Let me say that these things have all happened before in the anthroposophical movement, as if to illustrate the point, truly as if to illustrate the point. For instance, we were invited to a spiritualist society in Berlin[86] where I was to talk about anthroposophy. It did not occur to me to say no. Why should those people not have the right to hear something like that? I delivered my lecture and saw immediately afterwards that they were quite unsuited, that in reality they didn't want to hear anything more from me. For something happened after this lecture which turned out to be quite funny. I was elected immediately and unanimously as the president of this Society. Marie Steiner and her sister, who had accompanied me, were shocked. What should we do now? they asked. I had become president of this Society. What should we do? I simply said: Stay away! That was perfectly obvious. By electing as their president someone they had heard speak on only one occasion, those people showed that they wanted something quite different from anthroposophy. They wanted to infuse anthroposophy with spiritualism and thought that they could achieve it by this means. We come across that kind of thing all the time.

So it should never be a case of holding back from advocating anthroposophy before anyone. I was invited once to speak about anthroposophy to the Gottsched Society[87] in Berlin. Why should I not have done that? The important thing was not to compromise over the anthroposophical content.

That was particularly difficult after I had written the 'Appeal to the German People and the Civilized World', and after *Towards Social Renewal* had been published.[88] The essential thing at that time was to do nothing in any respect other than advocate what could be done on the basis of this source, and then to wait and see who wanted to participate.

I am convinced even today that if we had done that, if we had simply adopted the positive position which was contained in the 'Appeal' and in the book, without seeking links with any particular party—something which I was always against—we would not be stumbling today over obstacles which have been put in our way from this quarter, and would probably have been able to achieve one or two successes. Whereas now we have achieved no successes at all in this field, my dear friends.

It is part of the conditions governing the existence of a Society like ours that opportunities must always be found to work out of the spirit itself. That should not, of course, lead to the stupid conclusion that we have to barge in everywhere like bulls in china shops or that we do not have to adjust to the conditions dictated by life, that we should become impractical people; quite the contrary. It is necessary to inject some real practical life experience into the so-called practical life of today. Because to anyone who has some understanding of the conditions governing life itself, this life will appear—well, like the life of the 'really practical people',[89] who have such a practical attitude to life that they immediately trip over their own two feet as soon as they try to stand up. That is what many people today describe as practical life. If these people and their real life experience manage to penetrate a spiritual movement, things really begin to look bad for the latter.

As I said, today I would rather dwell on the positive side of the matter and not, as I have often done, criticize what has happened but just show how things should be done. We should not pursue a course so rigid that we run headlong into any obstacle in the way; of course we need to take avoiding action, make use of the things which will achieve practical progress. The important factor is that everything should contain the impulse which comes from the core.

If we could progress in this way, we would quickly see that the Anthroposophical Society would finally shed the image—not in any superficial or conventional way, but justifiably—which still makes it appear sectarian to other people.

What is the use of telling people repeatedly that we aren't a sect if we then behave as if we are one? For you see, the one thing which needs to be understood by the members of the Anthroposophical Society is the general conditions which govern the existence of a Society in our modern age. A Society cannot be sectarian. That is why, if the Anthroposophical Society is to stand on its proper ground, the 'we' should never play a role with regard to any views. Anthrop-osophists can repeatedly be heard to tell the outside world: We, the Society, have this or that view. Something or other is happening to us. We want one thing or another. That was possible in ancient times, that Societies faced the world with such conformity. Now it is no longer possible. In our time each person who is a member of a Society like this one has to be a really free human being. Views, thoughts, opin-ions are held only by individuals. The Society does not have an opin-ion. And that must already be expressed in the way that individuals speak about the Society. The 'we' should actually disappear.

There is something else connected with this. If this 'we' disappears, people in the Society will not feel as if they are in a pool which sup-ports them and which they invoke when it matters. But if a person has expressed their own views in the Society and has to represent themselves, they will also feel fully responsible for what they say as an individual.

This feeling of responsibility is something which has to grow as long as the Society remains a small group of people. The way in which that has been put into practice so far has not succeeded in making the world at large understand the Anthroposophical Society as an eminently modern Society, because this practice has repeatedly led to a situation in which the image which has been set before the public is *we* believe, *we* are of the opinion, it is *our* conception of the world. So today the world outside holds the view that the Society is a compacted mass which holds certain collective opinions to which one has to subscribe as a member. Of course this will deter any inde-pendently minded person.

Since this is the case, we have to consider a measure today which need not have been thought about, perhaps even a year ago. If things had not progressed that far, if at that time we were not yet tarred with the same brush as the Carbonari,[90] the Soviet government and

Irish republicanism—with certain ulterior motives, of course—it now seems necessary to think seriously about how the three objects[91] which are always being quoted as an issue might be put in context: fraternity without racial distinctions and so on, the comparative study of religions, and the study of the spiritual worlds and spiritual methodology. By listing these three objects, the impression is given to the world that one has to swear by them. A completely different form has to be found for them, above all a form which allows anyone who does not want to subscribe to a particular opinion, but who has an interest in the cultivation of the spiritual life, to feel that they need not commit themselves body and soul to certain points of view. That is what we have to think about today, because it belongs to the conditions governing the existence of the Society, having experienced the particular configuration of the third phase.

I have often been asked by people whether they would be able to join the Anthroposophical Society as they could not yet profess to the prescriptions of anthroposophy. I responded that it would be a sad state of affairs if a Society in today's context recruited its members only from among those who profess what is prescribed there. That would be terrible. I always said that honest membership should involve only one thing: an interest in a Society which in general terms seeks the path to the spiritual world; to have an interest in that. How that is done in specific terms is then the business of those who are members of the Society, with different contributions from all of them.

I can understand very well why someone would not want to be member of a Society in which they had to subscribe to certain articles of faith. But if we say that anyone can be a member of this Society who has an interest in the cultivation of the spiritual life, then those who have such an interest will come. And the others, well, they will remain outside, but they will be led increasingly into the absurdities of life.

No account is taken of the circumstances of the Anthroposophical Society until one starts to think about conditions such as these which govern its life, until one stops shuffling along in the same old rut. Only when the Society achieves the ability to deal with these issues in a completely free way, without pettiness and with generosity, will it be possible for it to become what it should become through the fact that it contains the anthroposophical movement. For the anthroposophical movement connects in a positive way, without compromise but in a positive way, to what exists in the present and what can act productively into the future.

It is necessary to develop such sensitivity towards these things. And it is necessary for anthroposophists to develop this sensitivity in, let me say, a matter of weeks. If that happens, the way forward will be found as a practical consequence.

But people will only be able to think in this direction if they radically discard the petty aspects of their character and truly begin to focus on what is important, begin to understand the need to recognize Anthroposophia as an independent, invisible being.

I have had to speak about the third period in a different way, of course, to the two preceding ones. The latter are already history. The third, although we are nearing its end, is the present and everyone should be aware of its circumstances. We have to work our way towards guidelines concerning the smallest details. Such guidelines are not dogma, they are simply a natural consequence.

Tomorrow I will present what remains to be said. We will then see whether we can conclude these lectures with that.

# LECTURE EIGHT

## DORNACH, 17 JUNE 1923

T ODAY we will have to reach some kind of conclusion in our deliberations. Clearly, and as was also mentioned already yesterday, that will have to include drawing the consequences which arise for the future action of the Anthroposophical Society. In order to gain a better understanding of what this action might be, let us take a look at the way anthroposophy emerged in modern civilization.

From the reflections of the last eight days, you will have realized how an interest in anthroposophy was at first to be found in those circles where the impulse for a deeper spiritual understanding was already present. This impulse came from all kinds of directions. In our context, however, it was only necessary to look at the way homeless souls were motivated by the material which Blavatsky presented to the present age in the form of what might be called a riddle.

So we have looked at that. But if the Anthroposophical Society can be traced back to this impulse, it should, on the other hand, also have become clear that this material was not central to anthroposophy itself. For anthroposophy as such relies on quite different sources. Even if the forms which were used to express the wisdom of anthroposophy used words at the beginning which were familiar to these homeless souls who came through their connection with Blavatsky—precisely because that audience came about as has been described—that is just what they were, forms of expression. If you go back to my early writings, *Christianity As Mystical Fact* and *Mystics after Modernism*, you will see that they are not based in any way on material which came from Blavatsky or from that direction in general, save for the forms of expression which were chosen to ensure that they were understood.

A distinction must be made between that which flowed through the anthroposophical movement as spiritual substance and that which initially had to be the form of expression because of the circumstances of the time. That errors can arise in this field is only due to the fact that people in the present day are so little inclined to go back from the outer form of expression to what is actually the essence of the matter. Anthroposophy goes back directly to the subject matter which is dealt with in philosophical terms in my *The Philosophy of Freedom*, as well as in my writings on Goethe of the 1880s.[92] If you examine that material, you will see that its essential point is that human beings are connected with a spiritual world in the most profound part of their being. If they therefore penetrate deeply enough into their own being, they will encounter something within themselves to which the natural sciences in their past and present form have no access, something which can only be seen as belonging directly to a spiritual world order.

Indeed, it should be recognized that it is almost inevitable that turns of phrase sometimes have to be used which might sound paradoxical, given the immense spiritual confusion of language which our modern civilization has produced. Thus it can be seen from my writings on Goethe[93] that it is necessary to modify our concept of love, if we are to progress from observation of the world to observation of the divine-spiritual. I indicated that the Godhead has to be thought of as having permeated all existence with eternal love and thus has to be sought in every single being, something quite different from any sort of vague pantheism. But there was no philosophical tradition in that period on which I could build. That is why it was necessary to seek this connection through someone who possessed a richer, more intense life, an inner life which was saturated with spiritual substance.

That was precisely the case with Goethe. When it came to putting my ideas in book form, I was therefore unable to build a theory of knowledge on what existed in contemporary culture, but had to link it with a Goethean world conception, and on that basis the first steps into the spiritual world were possible.

Goethe provides two openings into the spiritual world which give a certain degree of access, we might say. The first one is through his scientific writings. For the scientific view he developed overcomes an obstacle in relation to the plant world which is still unresolved in the whole of modern science. In his observation of the plant world he was able to substitute living, flexible ideas for dead concepts. Although he failed to translate his theory of metamorphosis into the animal world, it was nevertheless possible to draw the conclusion that similar ideas on a higher level not yet developed by Goethe could be applied to the animal realm. I tried to show in my *Goethe's Theory of Knowledge. An Outline of the Epistemology of His Worldview*[94] how it could have been possible to advance in outline to the level of history, historical life, with Goethe's revitalizing ideas. That was the one point of entry.

There is, however, no direct continuation into the spiritual world as such from this particular starting point in Goethe, but it is only possible to work up to a certain level from this there. But in working in this way we can have a feeling that we take hold of the world in a spiritual way. In applying Goethe's methodology, we are moving in a spiritual element. If we also apply this methodology to the plant world or animal world perceptible to the senses, then this enables us to understand the spiritual element active in the plant or the animal.

But Goethe also approached the spiritual world from another angle, from a perspective which he was able to indicate only through images, one might almost say symbolically. In his *Fairy Tale of the Green Snake and the Beautiful Lily*,[95] he wished to show how a spiritual element is active in the development of the world, how the individual spheres of truth, beauty and goodness act together, and how real spiritual beings, not mere abstract concepts, have to be grasped if we want to come to an understanding of the real life of the spirit.

It was thus possible to build on this element of Goethe's worldview. But that made something else all the more necessary. For the first thing we have to think about when we talk about a conception of the world which will satisfy the homeless souls is morality and ethics. In those ancient times in which human beings had access to the divine through their natural clairvoyance, it was taken for granted that moral impulses also came from this divine-spiritual principle to which they could ascend. If we look back to very ancient times in the development of humanity, the situation is such that human beings in their original primitive clairvoyance, let us say in the good old days, in looking up to the divine-spiritual raised their eyes to the essential forces which regulate the phenomena of nature. Natural phenomena, the action of the wind and the weather, of the earth and of mechanical processes, represented to these ancient human beings an extension of what they perceived as the divine-spiritual principle. But at the same time they also received the impulses for their own actions from that source. That is the distinguishing feature of this ancient view of the world, which was still connected with the primitive clairvoyance, that with regard to the ancient Egyptian period, say, people looked up to the stars in order to learn what would happen on earth; even to the extent of gaining insight into the conditions which governed the flooding of the Nile to support their needs. From the course of the stars, from the regularity of the stars, they derived that which interested them in the earthly world in its natural order. But by the same means they calculated, if I may use that term, what came to expression as moral impulses. Those, too, were derived from their observation of the stars.

If we look now to the modern situation, observation of the stars has become purely a business in which physical mathematics is simply transferred into the starry sky. And on earth so-called laws of nature are discovered and investigated. These laws of nature, which also Goethe already found, which he then transformed into living ideas, are remarkable in that the human being as such is excluded from the world if they are to adhere to the laws of nature, that the human being in their innermost being is no longer positioned in the world.

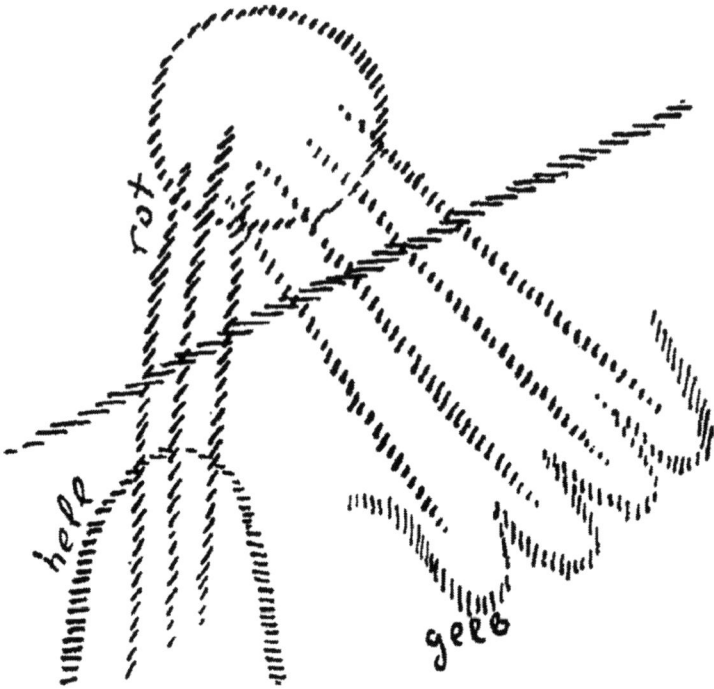

*rot = red; gelb = yellow; hell = light colouring*

If we think in diagrammatic form of the content of the old world conceptions, we have the divine-spiritual principle here on the one hand (red). The divine spirit penetrated natural phenomena. Laws were found for these natural phenomena, but they were recognized as something akin to a reflection of divine action in nature (yellow). Then there was the human being (light colouring). The same divine spirit (red) penetrated human beings. They received their substance, as it were, from the same divine spirit which also gave nature its substance.

What happened next? We have to look at what happened next in all seriousness. What happened next in a sense was that through natural science the link between nature and the divine was severed. The divine was removed from nature, and the reflection of the divine in nature began to be interpreted and talked about as the laws of nature.

For the ancients these laws of nature were divine thoughts. For modern people they are still thoughts, because they have to be grasped with thoughts, but they are explained on the basis of the natural phenomena which are governed by these laws of nature. People talk about the law of gravity, the law of the refraction of light, and lots of other fine things. But they have no real foundation, or rather no elevation, for the only way to give real meaning to these laws is to refer to them as a reflection of divine action in nature.

That is what the more profound person, the homeless soul, feels when we talk about nature today. It feels that those who talk about nature in such a superficial way deserve the Goethean—or, actually, the Mephisophelean—epithet: and mock themselves unwittingly.[96] People talk about the laws of nature, but the latter are remnants from ancient knowledge, a knowledge which still contained that additional element which underlies the natural laws.

Imagine a rose bush. It will flower repeatedly. When the old roses wither away, new ones grow. But if you pick the roses and allow the bush to die, you can't continue to keep having new roses. That is what has happened to the natural sciences. There was a rose bush with its roots in the divine. The laws which were found in nature were the individual roses. These laws, the roses, were picked. The rose bush was left to wither. Thus we have in our laws of nature something that is rather like roses without the rose bush: not a great deal of use to human beings. People simply fail to understand this in those clever heads of theirs, by which so much store is set in our modern times. But the people who are homeless souls do sense this a great deal in their hearts because the laws of nature mean nothing to them. They feel that these laws of nature wither away when they want to relate to them as human beings.

Modern humanity therefore unconsciously experiences the feeling, in so far as it still has the capacity to feel, in so far as it still has a heart in its body, that it is being told something about nature which withers the human being, which makes them wither. A terrible belief in authority forces people to accept this as pure truth. While they feel in their hearts that the roses are withering away, they are forced into a belief that these roses represent eternal truths. People talk about the eternal laws which underlie the world. Phenomena pass, but the laws are immutable. In the sense that anthroposophy represents what human beings want to develop from within themselves as their self-awareness, natural science represents anti-anthroposophy.

We need still to consider the other side, the ethical and moral. Ethical and moral impulses came from the same divine source. But just as the laws of nature were turned into withering roses, so moral impulses met the same fate. Their roots disappeared and they were left free-floating in civilization as moral imperatives of unknown origin. People could not help but feel that the moral commandments were there but their divine origin had been lost. And that raised the essential question of what would happen if they were no longer obeyed? Chaos and anarchy would reign in human society.

This was juxtaposed with another question: How do these commandments work? Where do we find their roots? Yet again, the sense of something withering away was inescapable. Goetheanism raised these questions, but they could not be answered from within Goetheanism. Goethe presented what I might call two starting-points which, although they moved in a convergent direction, never actually came together. *The Philosophy of Freedom* is, was, required for that.

It had to be shown where the divine is located in human beings, the divine which enables them to discover the spiritual basis of nature as well as of moral laws. That led to the concept of intuition presented in *The Philosophy of Freedom*, to what was called ethical individualism. Ethical individualism, because the source of the moral impulses in each single human individual had to be shown to reside in that divine element with which human beings are connected in their innermost being.

The time having arrived in which on the one hand a living understanding of the laws of nature and on the other hand of the moral commandments had been lost because the divine could no longer be found in the external world—it could not be otherwise in the age of freedom—it was necessary to find this divine-spiritual principle within human beings—because we encounter the human being in the first instance as an individual. But this produced a conception of the world which you will see, if you only consider it clearly, leads directly to anthroposophy.

Let us assume that we have human beings here. It is rather a primitive sketch but it will do. Human beings are connected with the divine spirit in their innermost selves (red). This divine-spiritual principle develops into a divine-spiritual world order (yellow). By observing the inner selves of all human beings in their interaction, we are able to penetrate the divine-spiritual sphere in the same way as the latter was achieved in ancient times by looking outward and seeing the divine spirit in physical phenomena, through primitive clairvoyance.

*rot = red; gelb = yellow*

In addition to what resulted on the one hand from the Goethean worldview and on the other simply from the necessities of human development at the end of the nineteenth century, our purpose must be to gain access to the spirit, not in an outer materialistic way, but through the real recognition of the essential human self.

Well, this is actually when anthroposophy came into being, if our observations are guided by life rather than by theoretical considerations. For if anyone argued that *The Philosophy of Freedom* was not yet anthroposophy it would be as if they were to say that there was a person called Goethe; this Goethe wrote a variety of works; we see Goethe today as the creator of his works. But then someone else replies: This is hardly a consistent view for a child born in Frankfurt am Main in 1749 who was blue at birth and not expected to live. If we look at everything connected with this child, Goethe's works cannot logically be deduced from that child. That is not being consistent. You have to trace Goethe back to his origins. See if you can find *Faust* in the blue boy born in Frankfurt am Main in 1749!

That is not a particularly clever standpoint, is it? It is just as silly to say that it is inconsistent to argue that anthroposophy developed from *The Philosophy of Freedom*. The blue child in Frankfurt continued to live and his life led to what today lives as Goethe in the development of the world. *The Philosophy of Freedom* had to continue to live and anthroposophy developed from it.

Just think if life were to be replaced by a philosophical logician who said that what is contained in *Faust*, in *Wilhelm Meister* and so on, must be logically deduced from the blue boy of 1749—do you think he would logically deduce anything? No, he would note contradictions, enormous contradictions. He would say: I can't reconcile what someone once wrote as *Faust* with what the blue boy in Frankfurt am Main was; that does not follow logically.

That is what those say who have nothing to do with life but with the dusty logic of school: anthroposophy does not logically follow from the *Philosophy of Freedom*.

If it followed logically, then just look how all the schoolmasters in 1894 would have deduced anthroposophy from the *Philosophy of Freedom*! But they kept well away from it. But afterwards they have to admit they cannot deduce it, they cannot make it work; they make it a contradiction between what comes later and what comes earlier. In our time, when we develop so-called logic, philosophy and so on, we do not have the ability to respond to life, to that which blossoms and grows, what goes beyond the pedantic practice of logic.

The task, then, was to make a critical assessment of those things in contemporary life which were endeavouring to bring progress to human civilization.

As you are aware, I tried to highlight two important phenomena for discussion. The first was Nietzsche. You will have seen from the previous reflections why this had to be, for in Nietzsche a personality came to the surface of more recent developments in our culture who grew into the way contemporary thinking was developing and who, in contrast to everyone else, was honest.

What did the others say? What was the general verdict, we might say, in the 1890s? The general verdict was that natural science was, of course, right. Natural science as it exists was a great authority. We stand on the terra firma of science and look up at the stars. There was the instance of the conversation between Napoleon and the great astronomer Laplace.[97] Napoleon could not understand how God was to be found by looking at the stars through a telescope. The astronomer responded that he didn't need such a hypothesis. And of course he didn't need it for observing the stars with a telescope. But he needed it from the moment that he wanted to be a human being. But the sight of the stars in the sky through a telescope gave nothing to humanity, nothing. The sky was full of stars, but full of stars for the senses, and otherwise it was empty.

Microscopes allowed the investigation of the smallest living entities and the smallest components of living entities and so on. Microscopes were made ever more perfect. But the soul was not found. You could look through a microscope for as long as you wished, but there was not the slightest trace of soul or spirit. The soul or the spirit could be found neither in the stars nor under the microscope. And so it went on. This is what Nietzsche came up against.

What did the others say? We look through a telescope at the stars and see worlds of the senses but nothing else. At the same time we also have a religious life, a religion which tells us that the spirit exists. David Friedrich Strauß[98] can drone on at length and draw the conclusion: Where can the spirit be found by scientific means? We maintain the position that the Scriptures that have been handed down to us speak about the spirit. We cannot find the spirit anywhere; but we profess our faith in its existence all the same. The science which we are committed to believe in is unable to find the spirit anywhere; it is the way it is because it seeks reality; if it were to take any other form it would be divorced from reality. In other words, anybody who undertakes a different kind of research will not find reality! Therefore we know about reality, and at the same time believe in something which cannot be established as a reality but which nevertheless, our forefathers tell us should be reality.

It was this which led a soul like Nietzsche's, which had maintained its integrity, to be torn apart. One day he realized he would have to draw the line somewhere. How did he do that? He did it by arguing that we have reality and reality is what is investigated by natural science. Everything else is invalid. Christianity teaches that Christ should not be sought in the reality which is investigated with the telescope and the microscope. But there is no other reality. As a consequence there is also no justification for Christianity. Therefore, Nietzsche said, I will write *The Anti-Christ*.

If you look through a microscope or a telescope you won't find any moral impulses. But people accept the moral commandments which are floating around or which authority tells us must be obeyed, but they cannot be discovered through scientific research. So in *Revaluation of All Values* Nietzsche wanted to write a second book after *Anti-Christ*, which was to be his first book, in which he showed that all ideals are actually worth nothing because they cannot be found in reality and should be abandoned.

And he wanted to write a third book. Moral principles certainly cannot be deduced from the telescope or the microscope, and so, Nietzsche said, I will establish amorality. Thus the first three books of *Revaluation of All Values* were to be called: first book, *Anti-Christ*; second book, *Nihilism or the Abolition of Ideals*; third book, *Amorality or the Abolition of the Universal Moral Order*.

It was something terrible, of course, but his standpoint took to its final and honest conclusion what had been started by others. We will not understand the nerve centres of modern civilization if we do not observe these things. It was something which had to be confronted. The enormous error of Nietzsche's thinking had to be demonstrated and corrected by returning to his premises, and then showing that they had to be understood as leading not into the void but into the spirit. The confrontation with Nietzsche[99] was thus a necessity.

Haeckel, too, had to be confronted in the same way.[100] Haeckel's thinking had pursued the approach of natural science to the evolution of sensory beings with a certain consistency. This had to be utilized in the way I described to you immediately in my very first reflections. I did this in the first anthroposophical lectures I ever gave, with the help of Topinard's book.[101] This kind of approach made it possible to enter the real spiritual world through living progress. The details could then be worked on through further research, through continuing to live with the spiritual world.

I have said all this in order to make the following point. If we want to trace anthroposophy back to its roots, it has to be done against a background of illustrations from modern life. When we look at the development of the Anthroposophical Society we need to keep in mind the question: Where were the people who had an incentive to understand matters of the spirit? They were the people who, because of the special nature of their homeless souls, were prompted by Blavatsky and theosophy to search for the spirit.

The Theosophical Society and anthroposophy went alongside one another at the beginning of the twentieth century simply because of existing circumstances. That development had been fully outgrown in the third stage, which began approximately in 1914, as I explained. No traces were left which harked back to the old times of theosophy. Nothing was left even as regards the forms of expression. Whereas in any case right from the beginning of the anthroposophical work the thrust had to be to lead spiritual reflections to the Mystery of Golgotha, to penetrating Christianity, the thrust in the other direction had to be to understand natural science by spiritual means. Only what I might call the mastery of those spiritual means, through which the presentation of true Christianity in our age would be enabled once again, fell into an earlier period. It starts in the first period and is particularly worked on in the second period.

The work which was to be done in the various directions really only emerged in the third stage, as I set out in the last few days. That is when people working in science found their way into the anthroposophical movement. These people working in science should take particular care, if we are to avoid the repeated introduction of new misunderstandings into the anthroposophical movement, to take full cognizance of the fact that we have to work from the central sources of anthroposophy. It is absolutely necessary to be clear about this.

I believe it was in 1908 that I made the following remarks in Nuremberg[102] in order to describe a very specific state of affairs.

Modern scientific experimentation has led to substantial scientific progress. The studies using experiments have brought an exceptional amount to light. That can only be a good thing, for spirituality is at work in such experiments in the form of spiritual beings. It is mostly the case, I said at the time, that the scientist goes to the laboratory and pursues their work according to the routines and methods they have learnt. But what I might call a whole group of spiritual beings are working alongside them, and it is these who actually bring about results; for the person standing at the laboratory bench only creates the conditions which allow such results to emerge gradually. If that were not the case, things would not have developed as they have in modern times.

For you see, whenever someone has discovered something, like for example Julius Robert Mayer on his travels, it is clothed in exceedingly abstract formulae. Others found even that incomprehensible. When over time Philipp Reis was driven to the telephone, the others again found it incomprehensible. There is actually a yawning gap today between what people understand and what is produced by research, because people do not have access to the spiritual impulses.

That is how things are. Let us return once more to that excellent person, Julius Robert Mayer.[103] Today he is acknowledged as an eminent scientist, but at school always came bottom. As a student at Tübingen University he came close to being advised to leave before graduating. He scraped through his medical exams, was recruited as a ship's doctor and took part in a voyage to India. It was a rough passage; many sailors on board became ill and he had to bleed them on arrival.

Now doctors know, of course, that there are two types of blood vessel: veins and arteries. Arterial blood spurts out red, venous blood spurts out with a bluer tinge. When a person is bled and an incision is made in the vein, bluish blood should therefore spurt out. Julius Robert Mayer had to bleed many people. But with all the sailors on board who were on the voyage, who had been through the turmoil at sea which made them sick, something peculiar happened when he made his incisions. He must have cursed inwardly, because he thought he had hit the wrong place, an artery, since red blood appeared to be spurting out of the vein. When he bled the next person, the same thing happened. He became quite confused because he thought every time that he had hit the wrong place. Finally he reached the conclusion that he had made his incisions in the right place after all but, as people had become sick at sea, something had happened to make the venous blood more red than blue, at least nearer the colour of arterial blood, when it spurted out.

Thus a modern person, who had not been taught to seek any kind of spiritual connections out of the spirit, inadvertently made a tremendous discovery while bleeding people. But what does he say? The modern scientist says: Now I have to think about what actually happened there. Energy is transformed into heat and heat into energy, as in the steam engine. You create heat and movement is brought about: activity, activity from heat, and something similar happens in people. And since a person is subject to different heat in the tropics, where the ship had sailed, they do not need to make that transformation into blue blood. In accordance with the law of the transformation of natural forces things happen differently. Other heat conditions prevail in the human organism: the blood does not turn as blue but it remains red in the veins.

The law, recognized today, of the transformation of matter, of forces is deduced from this observation.

Let us imagine that something similar was experienced by a doctor not, say, in the nineteenth but, if we think of different circumstances, in the eleventh or twelfth century if you like. They would never have thought to derive the mechanical concept of heat equivalence from such observed facts. It would never have occurred to them to link something as abstract as that to such a phenomenon. You can even think of later periods because Paracelsus,[104] for instance, would never have thought of it, not even in his sleep, although Paracelsus was much cleverer, even in sleep, than some others when they are awake. The doctor who would have been something like Paracelsus—and Julius Robert Mayer was for the nineteenth century what Paracelsus was for his age—a hypothetical doctor who, let us assume, lived in the tenth, eleventh, twelfth century if you like, what would he have said?

Van Helmont[105] speaks about the *archeus*, what today we would call the joint function of the etheric and astral bodies. We have to rediscover these things through anthroposophy, since such terms have been forgotten. The doctor in the twelfth century would have said: In the temperate zone, we have red and blue blood in the human being which strongly interact. When we get to a hotter climate, the difference between the venous and the arterial blood in the human being is no longer so pronounced; there the blue blood of the veins becomes redder and the red blood of the arteries bluer. There is no longer any great difference between them. What is the reason for that? The eleventh or twelfth century doctor would have said—and he would have used the term *archeus* or something similar at the time for what we describe as astral body today—that in the human being the *archeus* enters less deeply into the body in the hot zone than in the temperate zone. In the temperate zone human beings are more saturated, more densely permeated by their astral body; in the human being of the hot zone the astral body remains outside to a greater extent, even when they are awake. The consequence is that the differentiation in the blood which is caused by the astral body occurs more strongly in human beings in the temperate zone, less so in human beings in the hot zone. People in hotter climates therefore have freer astral bodies, which we can see in the lesser thickening of the blood. They live more instinctively in their astral bodies because it is freer. In consequence they do not become mechanistically thinking Europeans, but spiritually thinking Indians, who at the height of their civilization—not now that it has declined, but at the height of their civilization—have to have a different, a spiritual civilization, a Vedic civilization, while Europeans have to have the civilization of Comte, John Stuart Mill and Darwin.[106]

Such is the view of the *anthropos* which the eleventh or twelfth-century doctor would have derived from bleeding their patient. They would have had no problem with anthroposophy. They would have found access to the spirit, the living spirit. Julius Robert Mayer, the Paracelsus of the nineteenth century if you like, was left to discover the law: nothing can arise from nothing, so energy must be transformed; an abstract formula.

The spiritual element in the human being, which can be redis-covered through anthroposophy, also in turn leads to morality. We return full circle to the investigation of moral principles in *The Phi-losophy of Freedom*. Human beings are given entry to a spiritual world in which they are no longer faced with a division between nature and spirit, between nature and morality, but where the two form a union.

As you can see from what I have presented to you, the leading authorities in modern science arrive at abstract formulae. Such for-mulae buzz through the brains of those who today have had a scien-tific training. Those who give such a scientific training consider this tangle of abstract formulae as something in which people today have to believe. They regard as pure madness the claim that it is possible to progress from the qualities of red and blue blood to the spiritual element in human beings.

You can see from this what it takes if real scientists want to find their way into anthroposophy. Something more than mere good intentions is needed. They must have a real commitment to deepen-ing their knowledge to a degree to which we are not accustomed now-adays, least of all if we have had a scientific training. That requires courage, courage and more courage. And here we have come to the element we need above all for our soul if we want take into account the conditions governing the existence of the Anthroposophical Society. In certain respects the Society stands diametrically opposed to what is popularly acceptable in the world. It therefore has no future if it wants to make itself popular. Thus it would be wrong to court popularity, particularly in relation to our endeavours to intro-duce anthroposophical working methods into all areas of life, as we have attempted to do since 1919.[107] Instead, we have to pursue the path from the centre of its being which is based on the spirit itself, as I discussed here in this particular case this morning in relation to the Goetheanum.[108]

We must learn to adopt such an attitude in all circumstances, oth-erwise we begin to stray in a way which justifiably makes people con-fuse us with other movements and judge us by external criteria. If we are determined to provide our own framework we are on the right path to fulfilling the conditions which govern the existence of the anthroposophical movement. But we have to acquire the commitment which will then provide us with the necessary courage.

And we must not ignore those circumstances which arise from the fact that, as anthroposophists, we are a small group. As such we hope that what is spreading among us today will begin to spread among a growing number of people. Then knowledge and ethics, artistic and religious development will move in a new direction.

But all these things which will be present one day through the impulse of anthroposophy, and which will then be regarded as quite ordinary, must be cultivated to a much higher degree by those who make up the small group today. They must feel that they bear the greatest possible responsibility towards the spiritual world. It has to be understood that such an attitude will instinctively be reflected in the verdict of the world at large.

Nothing can do more harm, more profound harm to the Anthroposophical Society than the failure of its members to adopt a form which makes people outside aware in the strictest terms what anthroposophists are trying to achieve, so that they can be distinguished from all sectarian and other movements.

As long as this does not happen, it is not surprising that people around us judge us as they do. People don't know what the Anthroposophical Society stands for, and when they meet anthroposophists they see nothing of anthroposophy. You see, if anthroposophists were, say, recognizable by such a pronounced sensitivity to truth and reality that people notice: that is an anthroposophist, it is evident that they have such sensitive understanding that they go no further in their claims than accords with reality—that would indeed make an impression! But I do not want to criticize today but to emphasize only the positive side. Will it happen? That is the question we have to bear in mind.

Or alternatively people might say: Yes, those are anthroposophists; they don't allow themselves any display of bad taste, they have a certain artistic sense. The Goetheanum in Dornach must have had some effect. Once again people would know that anthroposophy provides its members with a certain modicum of taste which distinguishes them from others.

Such attitudes, you see, not the things that can be laid down in sharply defined concepts, must be among the things which are developed in the Anthroposophical Society if it is to fulfil the conditions governing its existence.

Such matters have been discussed a great deal! But the question which must always be in the forefront is how the Anthroposophical Society can be given that special character which will make people aware that here they have something which distinguishes it from others in a way which rules out any possibility of confusion. That is something anthroposophists should discuss at great length.

These things are a matter of conveying a certain feeling. Life cannot be constrained by programmes. But ask yourselves whether we have fully overcome the attitude within the Anthroposophical Society which dictates that something must be done in a specific way, which lays down rules; and whether there is a strong enough impulse to seek guidance from anthroposophy itself whatever the situation. That does not mean it has to have been said in a lecture, but what is said in lectures enters the heart, and that gives a certain guidance.

Until, my dear friends, and this is something I have to say here too, anthroposophy is taken as a living being who moves invisibly among us, towards whom we feel a certain responsibility, this small group of anthroposophists will not serve as a model. And that is what they should be doing.

Whenever you went into any of the Theosophical Societies, and there were many of them, they had the three famous objects. I spoke yesterday already about how we should view them. The first was to build a universal brotherhood of humanity without distinction of race, nationality and so on. I pointed out yesterday that we should be reflecting on the appropriateness of setting this down like a dogma.

It is, of course, important that such an object should exist, but it has to be lived. It must gradually become a reality. That will happen if anthroposophy itself is seen as a living, supersensory, invisible being who moves among anthroposophists. Then there might be less talk about brotherhood and universal human love, but they will live to a greater extent in human hearts. And then it will be evident in the tone in which people talk about their connection with anthroposophy, in the tone in which they talk to one another, that it is important to them that they too are followers of the invisible being of Anthroposophia.

After all, we could just as well choose another way. We could form lots of cliques and exclusive groups and behave like the rest of the world, meeting for tea parties or whatever, to make conversation and possibly assemble for the occasional lecture. That is also how we could do it. We can form small cliques and circles. But an anthroposophical movement could self-evidently not exist in such a Society. An anthroposophical movement can only live in an Anthroposophical Society which has become reality. But that requires a truly serious approach. It requires a sense of alliance in every living moment with the invisible being of Anthroposophia.

If that became a reality in people's attitude, not necessarily overnight but over a longer time span, an impulse would certainly develop over a period of perhaps twenty-one years. Whenever anthroposophists encountered the kind of material from our opponents which I read out yesterday for example, the appropriate response would come alive in their hearts. I am not saying that this would have to be transformed immediately into concrete action, but the required impulse would live in the heart. Then the action, too, would follow.

If such action does not develop, if it is only our opponents who are active and organized, then the right impulse is clearly absent. Then people clearly prefer to continue their lives in a comfortable fashion and listen to the occasional lecture on anthroposophy. But that is not enough if the Anthroposophical Society is to thrive. If it is to thrive, anthroposophy has to be alive in the Anthroposophical Society. And if that happens then something significant can develop over twenty-one years, or even over a shorter period. But by my calculations, the Society has already existed for twenty-one years.

However, since I do not want to criticize, I will only call on you to reflect on this issue to the extent of asking whether each individual, whatever their situation, has everywhere done everything with a feeling which is derived from the centre of anthroposophy?

If one or another among you should feel that this has not been the case so far, then I appeal to you: start tomorrow, start tonight for it would not be a good thing if the Anthroposophical Society were to collapse. But collapse it most certainly will if—now that the Goetheanum is being rebuilt in addition to all the outer reasons that already exist—that awareness of which I have spoken in these lectures does not develop, if such self-reflection is absent. And once the process of collapse has started, it will proceed very quickly. Whether or not it happens is completely dependent on the will of those who are members of the Anthroposophical Society.

Anthroposophy will certainly not disappear from the world. But it might very well sink back into what I might call a latent state for decades or even longer before it is taken up again. That, however, would imply an immense loss for the development of humanity. It is something which has to be taken into account if we are serious about engaging in the kind of self-reflection which I have essentially been talking about in these lectures. What I certainly do not mean is that we should once again make ringing declarations, set up programmes, and generally state our willingness to be absolutely available when something needs to be done. We have always done that. What is at stake here is that we should find the centre of our being within ourselves. If we engage in that search for the inner centre of our being in the spirit of wisdom transmitted by anthroposophy then we will also find the anthroposophical impulse which the Anthroposophical Society needs for its existence.

In these lectures in particular I have not wanted to be overly critical. A lot of criticism has, after all, been expressed recently, a lot has been said on various occasions. My intention has been to stimulate some thought about the right way to act by means of a reflection on anthroposophical matters and a historical survey of one or two questions; were I to deal with everything I would run out of time. And I believe these lectures in particular are a good basis on which to engage in such reflection, in what we might call such consideration. There is always time for that, because it can be done between the lines of the life, between the lines of the life which comes with the demands of the outer world.

That is what I wanted you to carry away in your hearts, rather like a kind of self-reflection for the Anthroposophical Society. We certainly need such self-reflection today. We should not forget that we can achieve a great deal by making use of the sources of anthroposophy. If we fail to do so then we abandon the path by which we can achieve effective action.

We are faced with major tasks, such as the reconstruction of the Goetheanum. In that context our heartfelt considerations should truly be based on really great impulses; we should not start from petty things. That is what I said this morning to those who were there, and that is what I wanted to put before you again this evening from a certain perspective.

# FOREWORD TO THE FIRST EDITION

T HE content of the lectures published here, given in a lively conversational and communicative tone and not intended as a book, may be taken as a supplement to what Rudolf Steiner presents us with in his book *Autobiography*. However, the exceedingly important content they contain and the whole historic context make them a document of inestimable value—and not only for the anthroposophist who in a luminous way can see the conditions and circumstances of the movement they have joined, so gaining firm ground under their feet through their insight into the necessity of these events that require no kind of justification; but those people, too, who otherwise hear only shallow judgements or find them printed in some reference book may also be grateful for this occasion to acquire a real insight into the facts. Surely there must be an ever increasing number of human souls who will eagerly seize such an opportunity to experience that an answer can be found to those questions which stand like the riddles of the Sphinx before the inner eye, and that the way to the answer can be actually shown them.

There is no longer any right for newspaper features and pamphlets to repeat that salvation in humanity's desperate plight would only be possible with the appearance of a universal genius, one who could master all the various branches of life and knowledge, co-ordinate and combine them, balance one with another, and then act in an innovative creative way; and that the only escape from uncertainty would be to break through the boundaries of knowledge, but that this is impossible...

For this genius has been here and *has* broken through the boundaries of knowledge. His work lies before us and bears testimony that he has done so. No word of his, however intimately uttered, need shun the light, and can be made accessible to everyone. The moral power, the transcendent elevation of his whole life and being shine forth from this work as luminously as the certainty of his all-embracing knowledge.

Why was no means spared to oppose him and render him harmless through slander when silence alone was no longer sufficient? Because our time does not tolerate the exceptional, hates it, does not want to admit its right to exist and thereby accommodates the powerful organizations that have an interest in not allowing that to arise which they themselves do not want to grant to humanity. They continue to prefer that idol of the present day, materialistic science. Goethe's words, which he dedicated to the insightful, remain true:

> Why, who dare give the child its proper name?
> The few who had some knowledge of these things,
> And, fool-like, set no guard on their full hearts,
> Revealed their feelings, visions, to the herd.
> —These from of old they crucified and burnt.[109]

No further explanation is needed for this hatred and destructive rage. It is the hatred that the world turns upon whatever is higher than itself. This hatred displays the face and works of the world's Adversary.

But now—when the excesses of this hatred can scarcely be further surpassed; when the great bearer of human liberation is dead; when the base and selfish motives of the fight have already become all too evident—now there will be increasing numbers of souls who will want to see through this tangle and trace the development of spiritual events, discover their source and first steps. Those who are interested in the historical development of the movement will find in this book the information they need, and will at the same time find the necessary explanation of and very simple reason for what arose as a matter of course out of the existing circumstances: the original association with the Theosophical Society which was looking for an initiated teacher. If a person is called upon and the conditions he lays down are accepted, why should he not go and help? If he is approached and does not shy away from drawing attention to the consequences of working together: the relearning process, the need to awaken to the demands of the time, the sensitivity to be developed for the progress of events and for the task of the West—why should the person who is certain of his path not seek to help those who were searching without a guide, show them the way to the divine guide and their own freedom?

If Annie Besant[110] had not been blinded at the most far-reaching moment of her life, when she lacked all certainty, everything could still have turned out well and she could have found the lost bridge to Christ without needing to manufacture the little substitute idol[111] who has now slipped through her fingers. With her, thousands in the Theosophical Society would have taken the path of inner liberation.

Rudolf Steiner alone threw a light on the riddle of Blavatsky;[112] she did not need to represent an obstacle for him because he saw the positive element in her work and managed to direct this positive element into channels where, freed from all its aberrations, delusions and chains, it could continue to be fruitful as powerful knowledge without doing any harm. Thus Blavatsky, in her progress as an individual, received her due thanks and had her karma eased. Her inner being—all that she was as an honest soul and strong force—will stand taller in history than if she remained intertwined with the spiritualistic phenomena that represent the difficult side of her karma. It was difficult to find one's way to what one sensed must be the core of her being when one heard the countless miracle tales that her intimate or more distant friends told about her, as happened to the writer of these lines. But one sensed a very significant power and greatness from reading even just a few pages of *Isis Unveiled* or *The Secret Doctrine,* which were of quite a different calibre from anything that was contained in the entire collection of books of the Theosophical Society. The key to her complicated nature was given to us by Rudolf Steiner and despite the very poor transcripts from 1915, as we did not yet have a professional stenographer in Dornach, it will be necessary to publish Rudolf Steiner's lectures on these mysterious phenomena, even if they are much mangled,[113] in order to shed more light on them.

HP Blavatsky was born in 1831. The centenary of her birthday falls in the present year. We may assume that many festivals and commemorations will be held by theosophists in all countries. Blavatsky was a child of nature, with a temperament of great native vigour. She had suffered much under the conventions of Anglo-American society so foreign to her nature; and to its representatives she was in turn merely a phenomenon, a semi-barbarian, not understood. Through her the adjacent world knocked at the door of the world shut off by materialism. Furthermore, she did not understand herself and suffered terribly each time she awoke from states that eluded her consciousness. Those will serve her memory best who understand her in the light and context of the first attempts by occultists to break the spell of materialism. Not to negate her accomplishments, connected as they may be with errors, but to rescue what is positive and preserve it for the future is the duty of the spiritually mature occultist. This is the light, too, in which the earlier collaboration of the Anthroposophical Society with the Theosophical Society must be understood, until the day when Annie Besant would no longer tolerate her own intentions being thwarted.

Although Rudolf Steiner tells us in these lectures that towards the end of the second stage the anthroposophical movement had outgrown everything which had come over to us as a legacy from the Theosophical Society, yet the fact remains that the influx of new generations and many theosophical members into our society has brought a constant recurrence of many symptoms which had previously been overcome and were not very pleasing, and which he made a great effort to cure. The result is that since people today are of the same kind as those who went before them, they must also go through the same mistakes and childhood illnesses—only, unfortunately, with an ever greater sense of self and stronger determination to live out their own foibles. What, after all, were the faults which Rudolf Steiner so censures in the lectures printed here—for example the adulation of Max Seiling[114] (a little local affair), or Bhagavân Dâs[115] (a passing fad)—compared to some of the things that have occurred in recent years? But he pointed to such symptoms to show their consequences, to expose the causes of these recurring signs of decline, and to show how Societies can fail when such behaviour enters the leading circles. At the time he considered the latter impossible with us. But he left us too soon; and among those who came to leadership too early, the old mistakes flared up—in a way that was human, all too human—with redoubled force.

It is incumbent on us to take stock of ourselves. Let us not make ourselves better than we are. There is no need to timidly hide our faults but we must let the light that brings self-knowledge shine in strength out of their darkness. Consciousness of the community is difficult; the development of a strong community I is only possible for us on the basis of the strength to wake up, the will for knowledge, the courage for truth. This cannot be achieved in secrecy; it must be fought for in community. Honest struggle will do us no harm, will bring us the respect of all those with goodwill. Those who are ill-disposed should think back to what the Church has suffered as a community despite the strongest outer discipline which it imposes; the extent to which its ideals had to suffer from flaws and contradictions. They will then see that the leader who gives the movement its impulses cannot be held responsible for the mistakes of those who follow his teachings, but that it is human beings as a species who cannot avoid the many detours, the climbing and backsliding, the renewed scramble upwards before they reach their goal.

Anthroposophy is a path of schooling. The Anthroposophical Society is certainly no model institution for how to live anthroposophical ideals. We might even say that in many respects it is an infirmary, which is not surprising in a time of human sickness. All those in need of help, all those who have been crushed by the need of our time flock towards it. But why should there only be infirmaries for the physically ill? Is there not a duty to have places where people can recover their spiritual equilibrium? That is what happened here in the widest sense. There have been a great many letters and words of gratitude in which people testified that it was only anthroposophy and its teacher who made life worth living for them once again. But in order for them to find anthroposophy there had to be a society in which such work was done.

Thus the Anthroposophical Society was a workshop in which an immense amount of work took place. Anthroposophy had a fertilizing influence in all areas of life: in the arts, the sciences, and also in practical endeavours. At the time of severe economic crisis, anthroposophists were frequently unable to realize the ideal that stood before them, but they were struggling against twice the odds. The people, however, who flocked to the Society and began to represent it to the outside when it was already somewhat established in the world in a representative way, were people moulded by our time rather than by corresponding to any ideal of anthroposophy, and thus many of them fell prey to the temptations and habits of the age.

The young people, who were disappointed by what they experienced and failed to find in the organized youth movements, here discovered the answers to the questions which were puzzling them, and sought to realize their endeavours in the new community of Anthroposophia; but they also brought their habits into the Society, including some things which should have been overcome by them if they wanted to make a fresh start in anthroposophy. And so the Anthroposophical Society cannot yet be a model institution; it remains a place of education. Do we not, however, need such places of schooling also in the wider context of humanity if we are to make progress towards a better future?

Whichever way we look at it, the Society is a necessity. It has to school itself and it has to provide the opportunity to be a place of education for humanity. The life forces with which it has been imbued can achieve this if strong, capable and devoted people gather together within it who know that it is necessary to join together in order as a community to service humanity in the wider sense; that they must not isolate themselves for the sake of self-indulgence; who know that it would be ingratitude simply to accept passively the lifeline which has been thrown; who know that with it comes the obligation to throw it to those others whose ship of life is in danger.

*Marie Steiner*
*1931*

# Notes

*Text sources:* These lectures, like almost all of Rudolf Steiner's lectures in Dornach and many others elsewhere after 1916, were taken down in shorthand by Helene Finckh. The volume is based on her own transcription into plain text.

The first edition was edited and provided with a Foreword by Marie Steiner in 1931; the second edition in 1959 was edited by H.W. Zbinden. The table of contents was expanded and the notes were supplemented for the 3rd edition in 1981.

[1]  *Bayreuther Blätter—Zeitschrift zur Verständigung über die Möglichkeit einer deutschen Kultur auf den Gebieten der Religion, Kunst, Philosophie und des Lebens.* Official organ of the Wagner Associations, established in 1878. Editor: Hans von Wolzogen.

[2]  See Rudolf Steiner, *Autobiography. Chapters in the Course of My Life, 1861–1907*, CW 28, as well as *Sämtliche Briefe 1*, Dornach 2021.

[3]  Fyodor Mikhailovich Dostoevsky, 1821–1881, leading Russian novelist. Cf. lecture of 13 February 1915 in *Die geistigen Hintergründe des ersten Weltkriegs*, GA 174b. Rudolf Steiner speaks in some detail about Dostoevsky's book *The Brothers Karamazov* in the lecture of 13 February 1916 in *The Human Spirit Past and Present*, CW 167.

[4]  Helena Petrovna Blavatsky, 1831–1891, referred to for short in theosophical circles as HPB. Her main works are *Isis Unveiled*, 1877, and *The Secret Doctrine*, 1887–97. Together with Col HS Olcott, Blavatsky founded the Theosophical Society on 17 November 1875 in New York, which soon thereafter moved its headquarters to India.

[5]  Alfred Percy Sinnett, 1840–1921. *Esoteric Buddhism*, 1883.

[6]  JW von Goethe. *Fairy tale of the Green Snake and the Beautiful Lily*. Floris Books, Edinburgh, 1979. Cf. Rudolf Steiner, *Goethes Geistesart in ihrer*

*Offenbarung durch seinen Faust und durch das Märchen von der Schlange und der Lilie* (1918), GA 22, as well as *Autobiography. Chapters in the Course of My Life, 1861–1907,* Chapter 30.

7   From 1890 to 1896/7 Rudolf Steiner was employed at the Goethe and Schiller Archive to edit Goethe's scientific writings within the Weimar edition of Goethe's works. Cf. Rudolf Steiner, *Autobiography. Chapters in the Course of My Life, 1861–1907,* Chapters 13–23, as well as *Sämtliche Briefe 1,* Dornach 2021.

8   1828–1901. Cf. *Autobiography. Chapters in the Course of My Life, 1861–1907.*

9   The article referred to is 'Eine vielleicht zeitgemäße persönliche Erinnerung' in the periodical *Das Goetheanum. Internationale Wochenschrift für Anthroposophie und Dreigliederung,* Vol. 2, No. 43 of 3 June 1923. Reproduced in *Der Goetheanum-Gedanke inmitten der Kulturkrisis der Gegenwart. Gesammelte Aufsätze 1921-1925,* GA 36.

10   *Unüberwindliche Mächte,* Berlin 1867.

11   In detail on 16 January 1913 in *Ergebnisse der Geistesforschung* (public lectures in Berlin, 1912/13), GA 62; as well as on 6 February 1915 in *Artistic Sensitivity as a Spiritual Approach to Knowing Life and the World,* CW 161.

12   The text of the preceding edition was not quite correct due to the inadequate transcript. It was corrected in line with the closing address of the first course of the School of Spiritual Science on 16 October 1920, in Rudolf Steiner, *Youth and the Etheric Heart,* CW 217a.

13   In the winter of 1900/1901, Rudolf Steiner delivered twenty-seven evening lectures in the Theosophical Library of Count and Countess Brockdorff. They were published as a collection in 1901 under the title *Die Mystik im Aufgang des neuzeitlichen Geisteslebens und ihr Verhältnis zur modernen Weltanschauung* (GA 7). They are published in English as *Mystics after Modernism. Discovering the Seeds of a New Science in the Renaissance,* CW 7. Cf. also *Autobiography. Chapters in the Course of My Life, 1861–1907,* Chapter 30.

14   Annie Besant, 1847–1933. Was elected in May 1907 to succeed HS Olcott as president of the Theosophical Society. Olcott had founded the Theosophical Society together with HP Blavatsky in New York in 1875.

15   Ralph Waldo Trine, 1866–1958. American author of philosophical books. Pupil of RW Emerson. His best known work is *In Tune with the Infinite* (New York, 1897).

16   The absurdities in the Theosophical Society referred to by Rudolf Steiner, which began to circulate in about 1910/11 and which culminated in

Annie Besant promoting the then 13/14-year-old boy Krishnamurti as the returned Christ through the newly founded organization 'Star of the East', were unanimously rejected by the Central European, German Section. This led to an organized attempt to suppress the Central European movement represented by Rudolf Steiner which ended with the resolution of the General Council in Adyar of 7 March 1913 to expel the German Section. Since this result was to be expected, the Anthroposophical Society had been founded on 28 December 1912 with an executive council comprising Dr Carl Unger, Michael Bauer and Marie von Sivers (Marie Steiner).

[17] This principle, enunciated by Goethe, was chosen by Rudolf Steiner as the motto for the principles which he gave to the Anthroposophical Society in 1912. From: 'Sprüche in Prosa', *Goethes Naturwissenschaftliche Schriften*, edited by Rudolf Steiner, Dornach 1975, Vol. V, p. 360.

[18] Rudolf Steiner, *The Philosophy of Freedom. The Basis for a Modern World Conception*, CW 4.

[19] Karl Wilhelm Ferdinand Solger, 1780–1819, philosopher and aesthetician.

[20] 1817. *Encyclopedia of Philosophy*. Philosophical Library, New York, 1959. Part One: Logic.

[21] Robert Zimmermann, 1824–1912. Philosopher and aesthetician. From 1861 to 1895 professor of philosophy at the University of Vienna. One of the leading representatives of Herbartian philosophy. Cf. Rudolf Steiner, *Autobiography. Chapters in the Course of My Life, 1861–1907*, Chapter 3.

[22] Franz Hartmann, 1838–1912. Physician and theosophist. Founder of a separate school within the Theosophical Society. Cf. Rudolf Steiner, *Autobiography. Chapters in the Course of My Life, 1861–1907*, Chapter 9, as well as *Briefe I*.

[23] *Geschichte der Aesthetik als philosophische Wissenschaft*, Vienna 1858. *Anthroposophie im Umriss—Entwurf eines Systems idealer Weltansicht auf realistischer Grundlage*, Vienna 1882. The text of the dedication referred to later on is as follows: To Harriet. It was your strength of soul, when night threatened to blanket my eyes, which made me resolve to use the long and involuntary leisure in my dark room to bring an ordered conclusion to a stream of thoughts long maturing in isolation, for which a willing hand kindly lent itself to write them down. Thus is the origin of this book of whose content no one will be able to dispute that, like the light, it was born in the dark. Who else but you could lay claim to the same?

24 Paul Topinard, 1830–1911. French anthropologist. A German translation of his *Anthropology* appeared in 1888.

25 The date and title could not be established.

26 The name 'Die Kommenden' was used by a society founded in Berlin by the poet Ludwig Jacobowski which consisted of literary figures, artists, scientists and others with an interest in the arts. Rudolf Steiner delivered 24 lectures from October 1901 to March 1902. Cf. also Rudolf Steiner, *Autobiography. Chapters in the Course of My Life, 1861–1907*, Chapters 29 and 30.

27 In the same winter, from October 1901 to April 1902, Rudolf Steiner again delivered a series of lectures in the Theosophical Library (see Note 13) which provided a comprehensive expansion of the subject treated in the previous year (mysticism). In 1902 these lectures were published as *Christianity As Mystical Fact*, CW 8.

28 Cf. Rudolf Steiner, *Eine historische Antwort*. From an address on 14 December 1911, reprinted in *Aus dem Leben von Marie Steiner-von Sivers*. Dornach, 1956. See also *Briefe II*.

29 The reference is to the second major lecture cycle of 27 lectures from October 1902 to April 1903 which was given to the Society Die Kommenden under the title 'From Zarathustra to Nietzsche. History of the development of humanity with reference to the worldviews from oldest oriental times to the present, or anthroposophy'. Rudolf Steiner had to leave the inaugural meeting of the German Section of the Theosophical Society, which took place on 20 October 1902 in the presence of Annie Besant, early for the third of these lectures, something he always expressly refers to in his reflections on the history of the anthroposophical movement. Cf. also *Autobiography. Chapters in the Course of My Life, 1861–1907*, Chapter 30.

30 Der Kommende Tag. Aktiengesellschaft zur Förderung wirtschaftlicher und geistiger Werte, established in Stuttgart on 13 March 1920. See Emil Leinhas, *Die Idee des Kommenden Tages*, Stuttgart 1921, as well as *Aus der Arbeit mit Rudolf Steiner*, Basel 1950, and Hans Kühn, *Dreigliederungszeit. Rudolf Steiners Kampf für die Gesellschaftsordnung der Zukunft*, Dornach 1978.

31 Friedrich Wilhelm Joseph Schelling, 1775–1854. *Die Weltalter*, a fragment from his unpublished works; English translation *The Ages of the World*. Columbia University Press, New York, 1942. *Philosophie der Offenbarung*, 2

Vols, Stuttgart/Augsburg 1858. Cf. the chapter 'The Classics of World and Life Conceptions' in Rudolf Steiner, *The Riddles of Philosophy* (1914), CW 18, p. 151–164. Cf. also the lecture in Dornach on 16 September 1924, in *Karmic Relationships*, Vol. 4, CW 238.

[32] See Note 42.

[33] Lawrence Oliphant, 1829–1888. His two most important books are *Symp-neumata* and *Scientific Religion*, London 1888. Cf. Rudolf Steiner's lecture in London on 24 August 1924, in *Karmic Relationships*, Vol. 6, CW 240.

[34] These are the so-called Mahatma Letters which were printed in AP Sin-nett's *The Occult World*, London, 1881. They are linked with the subsequent so-called Coulomb affair, which is what Rudolf Steiner is referring to when he speaks about 'a rather sensational affair', and 'all kinds of deceptively constructed sliding doors'.

[35] Simon Ohm, 1787–1854. Important physicist.

[36] Philipp Reis, 1834–1874. Teacher and physicist.

[37] Adalbert Stifter, 1805–1868. Writer and painter. The episode concerning his discovery as a writer by Baroness Mink in 1840 and his later appointment as schools' inspector in 1849/50 is recounted in every biography. Cf. for example Alois R Hein, *Adalbert Stifter, sein Leben und seine Werke*, Vienna/Zurich 1952, Vol. I, p. 141 and p. 326.

[38] Julius Robert Mayer, 1814–1878. Doctor and physicist.

[39] Ignaz Semmelweis, 1818–1884. Doctor, obstetrician, pioneer of antisepsis.

[40] Cf. Dornach, 11 October 1915 in *The Occult Movement in the Nineteenth Century* ..., GA 254; Berlin, 23 October 1911 in *Earthly and Cosmic Man*, GA 133; address in Helsingfors, 11 April, 1912 in *Our Connection with the Elemental World*, CW 158.

[41] Carl Gustav Jung, 1875–1961. Leading proponent of psychoanalysis. Cf. also Rudolf Steiner's lectures of 10 and 11 November 1917 in *Freud, Jung, and Spiritual Psychology*, CW 178; as well as the question-and-answer session related to the lecture of 28 April 1920 in *The Renewal of Education*, CW 301.

[42] Jakob Boehme, 1575–1624. Cf. Rudolf Steiner, *Mystics after Modernism*, CW 7. About the biographical event of the revelation at the sight of a pewter bowl, see Abraham von Frankenberg, 'Lebensbeschreibung Jakob Böhmes', § 11, in *Schriften Jakob Böhmes*, edited by H. Kayser, Leipzig 1920.

43  Dr Bruno Wille, author of *Offenbarungen des Wacholderbaums*, Novel of a
    Seer. Leipzig, 1901. Cf. Rudolf Steiner's detailed review in the journal
    *Luzifer* (Nos. 2 and 3, August and September 1903), reprinted in *Luzi-
    fer-Gnosis* (1903–1908), GA 34. Also *Autobiography. Chapters in the Course
    of My Life*, Chapter 29, and *Briefe II*.

44  The reference is to the lecture 'Monismus und Theosophie' of 8 Octo-
    ber 1902, extracts of which were reported in *Veröffentlichungen aus dem
    literarischen Frühwerk*, Vol. IV: *Anthroposophie und Seelenkunde*, Dornach
    1941. Cf. also *Autobiography. Chapters in the Course of My Life, 1861–1907*,
    Chapter 29, and *Briefe II*.

45  1857–1906. Poet and writer. His essay 'Hegels Phänomenologie des
    Geistes und die Theosophie' was published in the journal *Luzifer*, Vol. 1
    (1903), Issue 5, edited by Rudolf Steiner. Cf. Also *Autobiography. Chapters
    in the Course of My Life, 1861–1907*, Chapter 29, and *Briefe II*.

46  The name was not precisely heard by the stenographer.

47  Friedrich Nietzsche, 1844–1900. *The Anti-Christ*. See Rudolf Steiner,
    *Friedrich Nietzsche. Fighter for Freedom* (1895), GA 5.

48  'Was heißt und zu welchem Ende studiert man Universalgeschichte?',
    1789.

49  Rudolf Steiner: *The Gospel of St. John* (Hamburg 1908), CW 103; *The Gos-
    pel of St. John and its Relation to the Other Gospels* (Kassel 1909), CW 112;
    *According to Luke* (Basel 1909), CW 114; *According to Matthew* (Bern 1910),
    CW 123; *The Gospel of St. Mark* (Basel 1912), CW 139; *Background to the
    Gospel According to St. Mark* (Berlin and other places 1910/11), CW 124.

50  Published in 1897.

51  *Theosophy. An Introduction to the Supersensible Knowledge of the World and the
    Destination of Man* (1904), CW 9.

52  From 18–21 May 1907 the fourth annual Congress of the Federation of
    European Sections of the Theosophical Society took place in Munich.
    Under Rudolf Steiner's guidance the attempt had been made to create a
    harmonious correlation between the spiritual activity in and the artistic
    arrangement of the conference room. In addition there was a perfor-
    mance of Édouard Schuré's reconstruction of *The Holy Drama of Eleusis*.
    See *Autobiography. Chapters in the Course of My Life, 1861–1907*, Chapter
    38; also *Rosicrucianism Renewed. The Unity of Art, Science and Religion: The
    Theosophical Congress of Whitsun 1907*, CW 284.

[53] In the lecture of 14 December 1911 Rudolf Steiner declared that 'Annie Besant said in Munich in 1907 in front of a witness [Marie von Sivers] who is willing to testify to this at any time that she was not qualified to deal with Christianity. And that is why she, as it were, handed the movement over to me, in so far as its Christian aspects were concerned.' See *Aus dem Leben von Marie Steiner-von Sivers*, Dornach 1956, p. 45f.

[54] This refers to a lecture at the congress of the Theosophical Society in London in July 1902: 'Theosophy and Imperialism', A Lecture by Annie Besant, London (Theos. Publ. Soc.). Cf. Rudolf Steiner's lecture of 12 March 1916 in *Die geistigen Hintergründe des Ersten Weltkrieges*, GA 174b.

[55] See Note 16.

[56] See *Aus dem Leben von Marie Steiner-von Sivers*, Dornach 1956, p. 70f.

[57] See Note 16.

[58] *Occult Science: An Outline*, CW 13, had been announced in 1905 as a continuation of *Theosophy*, CW 9, which was published in 1904. For technical reasons, however, it did not appear until 1910 (the Preface is signed: written in December 1909). 'Only the absolute necessity of uninterrupted lecturing activity by the author has delayed the publication of this book for so long. Now it is to be made available to the public come what may.' (Rudolf Steiner in the journal *Luzifer-Gnosis*, No. 33 from 1907.)

[59] See Note 22.

[60] William Quan Judge, 1851–1896. One of the co-founders of the Theosophical Society. In 1895 he split away from the Adyar-based Society and became the leader of a secessionist movement in America.

[61] August Weismann, 1834–1914. Medical doctor, zoologist. Disputed the heredity of acquired changes.

[62] Dr Wilhelm Hübbe-Schleiden, 1846–1916. From 1886–1896 edited the occultist monthly journal *Sphinx*. See Rudolf Steiner, *Autobiography. Chapters in the Course of My Life, 1861–1907*, Chapter 32, and *Briefe II*.

[63] Charles Webster Leadbeater, 1847–1934. Prominent member of the Theosophical Society in England. See in this context the book *Occult Chemistry* by Annie Besant and CW Leadbeater, a series of clairvoyant observations about the chemical elements and atomic theory.

[64] Dr Eugen Kolisko, 1893–1939. Physician and teacher at the Stuttgart Waldorf School.

[65] The scientific research institute was one of the sections of Kommende Tag, a company set up for the promotion of economic and spiritual values, Stuttgart 1920–1925. The biology department (L Kolisko) was transferred to the Goetheanum by Rudolf Steiner in 1924.

[66] Helene von Schewitsch, née von Dönniges, 1845–1911; see Rudolf Steiner *Autobiography. Chapters from the Course of My Life, 1861–1907*, Chapter 38.

[67] Dr Ernst Blümel, 1884–1952. Mathematician and teacher, first in further education at the Goetheanum (Friedwart School) and subsequently (1927–1938) at the Waldorf School in Stuttgart.

[68] The journal appeared from June 1903 to 1908. Cf. *Autobiography. Chapters in the Course of My Life, 1861–1907*, Chapter 32. Rudolf Steiner's essays in *Luzifer-Gnosis* have been reprinted in the volume of the same name in the Complete Works, GA 34.

[69] See *Aus dem Leben von Marie Steiner-von Sievers*, Dornach 1956, p. 40ff.

[70] *The Spiritual Guidance of the Individual and Humanity* (1911), CW 15.

[71] *The Portal of Initiation* (1910), *The Soul's Probation* (1911), *The Guardian of the Threshold* (1912), *The Soul's Awakening* (1913): in Rudolf Steiner, *Four Mystery Dramas*, CW 14.

[72] Member of the Anthroposophical Society for a time. He turned against it when a book which he wanted to have published by Philosophisch-Anthroposophischer Verlag had to be turned down. See Rudolf Steiner's lecture of 11 May 1917 in *Die geistigen Hintergründe des Ersten Weltkrieges*, GA 174b.

[73] Prominent member of the Theosophical Society. Resigned his office as general secretary of the Indian Section in 1912 because he 'disapproved of the goings-on within the Order of the Star of the East in connection with the Krishnamurti-Alcyone cult, and of the behaviour of the president of the T.G. who approved of and encouraged these events unworthy of the Theosophical Society.' Cf. *Mitteilungen für die Mitglieder der Anthroposophischen Gesellschaft*, No. II, June 1913.

[74] The first congress of the Federation of European Sections of the Theosophical Society took place in Amsterdam in June 1904. Rudolf Steiner, as general secretary of the German Section, gave the lecture 'Mathematics and Occultism' there, in Rudolf Steiner, *Philosophie und Anthroposophie*, GA 35.

[75] Henry Steel Olcott, 1832–1907. Founder president of the Theosophical Society. See Rudolf Steiner, 'Henry Steel Olcott (an Obituary)', in the

journal *Luzifer-Gnosis*, No. 33 (March or April 1907). Olcott had proposed Annie Besant as his successor. Some of the circumstances surrounding this nomination had become public, which is why Rudolf Steiner wrote in the article 'Zur bevorstehenden Präsidentenwahl der Theosophischen Gesellschaft' (On the forthcoming election of the president of the Theosophical Society) (*Luzifer-Gnosis*, No. 33) as follows:

'... The deceased president did not merely state that he nominated Mrs Besant as his successor, but he informed the general secretaries through a variety of circulars—which then found their way into the theosophical press and, unfortunately, beyond—that the elevated individuals who are described as the Masters, and those in particular who are especially connected with theosophical affairs, had appeared at his death bed and had instructed him to nominate Mrs Besant as his successor. ... Now this addition to Mrs Besant's nomination could simply have been ignored. For whether or not one believes that the Masters genuinely appeared in this case, the source of Olcott's advice has no relevance to the members casting their vote in accordance with the Statutes. Whether he was advised by the Masters or by some ordinary mortals is his business alone. The voters have to adhere to the Statutes and solely ask themselves whether or not they consider Mrs Besant to be the right choice. An immediate difficulty arose, however, through the fact that Mrs Besant announced that she had been called upon by her Master to accept her nomination and that for this reason she would assume the burden; indeed, that she considered the order from the Masters as decisive in determining the outcome of the election. Objectively that is a disaster ... There would have been no reason to write these lines if the affair were not being discussed so much outside Germany. But under the circumstances the readers of this journal can rightly demand that it should not keep silent about a matter which is the subject of so much debate elsewhere.'

[76] CW Leadbeater (see Note 63) left the Theosophical Society in 1906 after the emergence of serious differences between him and the Society. But in 1909 he was re-admitted by Annie Besant, despite her earlier condemnation of his methods. In 1916, Leadbeater was consecrated as a bishop in the Liberal Catholic Church.

[77] In 1921, Rudolf Steiner spoke on 22 February about 'The Dornach building concept' and on 28 February about 'Education, teaching and

practical life questions from the perspective of anthroposophical spiritual science'.

[78] The person concerned was James Ingall Wedgwood. See Emily Lutyens, *Candles in the Sun,* London 1957.

[79] *The Secret Machinery of Revolution,* by G.G., London (1923, Reprinted from *The Patriot.*)

[80] Died 27 February 1784. Cf. also among others the lecture by Rudolf Steiner of 4 November 1904 in Berlin in *The Temple Legend,* CW 93.

[81] Marie Steiner had been involved with eurythmy from its beginnings in 1912 and took over the practice and development of Rudolf Steiner's indications from 1914 onwards. See *Aus dem Leben von Marie Steiner-von Sivers,* Dornach 1956, p.74ff.

[82] German: *Gedanken während der Zeit des Krieges. Für Deutsche und diejenigen, die nicht glauben, sie hassen zu müssen* (1915), reprinted in *Aufsätze über die Dreigliederung des sozialen Organismus und zur Zeitlage 1915 bis 1921,* GA 24.

[83] The courses for theologians (Stuttgart, 12–16 June 1921; Dornach, 26 September–10 October 1921; Dornach 6–22 September 1922) have not been published.

[84] Carl Unger, 1878–1929. Engineer. One of the most effective advocates of anthroposophy in Germany. Member of the executive council of the Anthroposophical Society from 1912 to 1923. A few moments before he was due to deliver his public lecture 'What is anthroposophy?' in Nuremberg, he was fatally shot by a mentally deranged person. See his book *Die Grundlehren der Geisteswissenschaft.* Dornach 1929.

[85] In the sense of 'factual' matters. In the previous edition it erroneously said 'more rhetorical'.

[86] It has not been possible to establish when this incident took place.

[87] On 17 October 1904. There is no transcript.

[88] The Appeal was printed in Stuttgart in 1919 and distributed as a leaflet with the signatures of many well-known personalities from German-speaking culture. Rudolf Steiner further included it in his book *Towards Social Renewal* (1919), GA 23. See also *Conscious Society. Anthroposophy and the Social Question* (Dornach 1919), CW 189.

[89] Title of a poem from the *Gallows Songs* by Christian Morgenstern, which is often presented in eurythmy.

90 Literally: charcoal burners. Name of a secret political society in Italy which was connected with Freemasonry and which also established a strong presence in France in the nineteenth century.

91 The reference is to the three objects of the Theosophical Society: 1. To form a nucleus of the universal brotherhood of humanity without distinction of race, creed, sex, caste or colour. 2. To encourage the study of comparative religion, philosophy and science. 3. To investigate unexplained laws of nature and the powers latent in humanity.

92 *Goethes Naturwissenschaftliche Schriften* with introductions and commentaries, edited and with commentaries by Rudolf Steiner, in *Kürschners Deutsche National-Literatur*, 5 volumes, 1883–1897. The introductions have been published separately as *Goethean Science. Introductions to Goethe's Natural-Scientific Writings*, CW 1. See also Rudolf Steiner, *Goethe's Theory of Knowledge. An Outline of the Epistemology of His Worldview* (1886), CW 2.

93 See for example *Goethean Science. Introductions to Goethe's Natural-Scientific Writings*, CW 1, Chapter 11 'The Relationship of the Goethean Way of Thinking to Other Views'.

94 See Note 92.

95 See Note 6. See also *Goethes Märchen von der grünen Schlange und der schönen Lilie* with nine drawings by Assia Turgenieff, drawn according to a chiaroscuro technique set out by Rudolf Steiner, Dornach 1929.

96 *Faust* I, 'Study', line 1941.

97 1749–1827. Unfortunately could not be verified.

98 1808–1874, Protestant theologian. See in this context his book *Der alte und der neue Glaube. Ein Bekenntnis*, Leipzig 1872 (e.g. Section III: 'Wie begreifen wir die Welt').

99 Rudolf Steiner. *Friedrich Nietzsche. Ein Kämpfer gegen seine Zeit* (1895), GA 5.

100 See Rudolf Steiner's lecture in Berlin, 5 October 1905, 'Haeckel, die Welträtsel und die Theosophie' in *Die Welträtsel und die Anthroposophie*, GA 54; also 'Haeckel und seine Gegner', 'Ernst Haeckel und die "Welträtsel"' and 'Die Kämpfe um Haeckels "Welträtsel"' in *Methodische Grundlagen der Anthroposophie 1884-1901*, GA 30, pp. 152, 391 and 441.

101 See p. 26 and Note 24.

102 In 1907 und 1908 Rudolf gave public lectures in various cities—in Nuremberg on 1 December 1907—on the subject of 'Science at the crossroads' of which mostly no or not very good transcripts exist. The

state of affairs described belongs to the subject matter covered in these lectures but could not be verified in greater detail.

[103] See Note 38. Cf. *Kleinere Schriften und Briefe von Robert Mayer nebst Mitteilungen aus seinem Leben,* edited by Weyrauch, Stuttgart 1893. Also Weyrauch, *Robert Mayer,* Stuttgart 1890.

[104] Theophrastus Bombastus Paracelsus von Hohenheim, 1493–1541. Cf. Rudolf Steiner's lecture in Berlin on 26 April 1906, 'Paracelsus', in *Die Welträtsel und die Anthroposophie,* GA 54 and *Mystics after Modernism* (1901), CW 7.

[105] Johann Baptist van Helmont, 1577–1644. Great Dutch doctor and philosopher. His works appeared under the title *Ortus medicinae,* Amsterdam 1648, and *Opuscula medica inaudita,* Cologne 1644.

[106] Auguste Comte, 1798–1857, positivist philosopher. John Stewart Mill, 1806–1873, philosopher, logician of empiricism. Charles Darwin, 1809–1882.

[107] A detailed list of the institutions in the fields of science, education, special needs education, medicine, publishing, the economy, and theology which were established on the basis of anthroposophy can be found in *Die Konstitution der Allgemeinen Anthroposophischen Gesellschaft,* GA 37/260a, p.712–724. Cf. also the lecture in Dornach on 2 March 1923 in *Awakening to Community,* CW 257.

[108] At the tenth general meeting of the Goetheanum Association on 17 June 1923 in Dornach. Reproduced in *Aufbaugedanken und Gesinnungsbildung.* Dornach 1942.

[109] *Faust I,* 'Night', lines 588–593.

[110] 1847–1933, president of the Theosophical Society since 1907. See Note 14.

[111] The reference is to Jiddu Krishnamurti, born 1897. See Note 16 as well as Emily Lutyens, *Candles in the Sun,* London 1957.

[112] See Note 4.

[113] The reference is to the ten lectures, which were not very well taken down in shorthand, given in Dornach from 10 to 25 October 1915, *Die okkulte Bewegung im neunzehnten Jahrhundert und ihre Beziehung zur Wewltkultur,* GA 254 (extended by three lectures).

[114] See Note 72.

[115] See Note 73.

# Rudolf Steiner's Collected Works

T HE German Edition of Rudolf Steiner's Collected Works (the *Gesamtausgabe* [GA] published by Rudolf Steiner Verlag, Dornach, Switzerland) presently runs to 354 titles, organized either by type of work (written or spoken), chronology, audience (public or other), or subject (education, art, etc.). For ease of comparison, the Collected Works in English [CW] follows the German organization exactly. A complete listing of the CWs follows with literal translations of the German titles. Other than in the case of the books published in his lifetime, titles were rarely given by Rudolf Steiner himself, and were often provided by the editors of the German editions. The titles in English are not necessarily the same as the German; and, indeed, over the past 75 years have frequently been different, with the same book sometimes appearing under different titles.

For ease of identification and to avoid confusion, we suggest that readers looking for a title should do so by CW number. Because the work of creating the Collected Works of Rudolf Steiner is an ongoing process, with new titles being published every year, we have not indicated in this listing which books are presently available. To find out what titles in the Collected Works are currently in print, please check our website at www.rudolfsteinerpress.com (or www.steinerbooks.org for US readers).

## Written Work

CW 1    Goethe: Natural-Scientific Writings, Introduction, with Footnotes and Explanations in the text by Rudolf Steiner

CW 2    Outlines of an Epistemology of the Goethean World View, with Special Consideration of Schiller

CW 3    Truth and Science

CW 4    The Philosophy of Freedom

CW 4a   Documents to 'The Philosophy of Freedom'

CW 5    Friedrich Nietzsche, A Fighter against His Time

## Public Lectures

## Lectures to the Members of the Anthroposophical Society

| CW 278 | Eurythmy as Visible Song |
| CW 279 | Eurythmy as Visible Speech |
| CW 280 | The Method and Nature of Speech Formation |
| CW 281 | The Art of Recitation and Declamation |
| CW 282 | Speech Formation and Dramatic Art |
| CW 283 | The Nature of Things Musical and the Experience of Tone in the Human Being |
| CW 284/285 | Images of Occult Seals and Pillars. The Munich Congress of Whitsun 1907 and Its Consequences |
| CW 286 | Paths to a New Style of Architecture. 'And the Building Becomes Human' |
| CW 287 | The Building at Dornach as a Symbol of Historical Becoming and an Artistic Transformation Impulse |
| CW 288 | Style-Forms in the Living Organic |
| CW 289 | The Building-Idea of the Goetheanum: Lectures with Slides from the Years 1920–1921 |
| CW 290 | The Building-Idea of the Goetheanum: Lectures with Slides from the Years 1920–1921 |
| CW 291 | The Nature of Colours |
| CW 291a | Knowledge of Colours. Supplementary Volume to 'The Nature of Colours' |
| CW 292 | Art History as Image of Inner Spiritual Impulses |
| CW 293 | General Knowledge of the Human Being as the Foundation of Pedagogy |
| CW 294 | The Art of Education, Methodology and Didactics |
| CW 295 | The Art of Education: Seminar Discussions and Lectures on Lesson Planning |
| CW 296 | The Question of Education as a Social Question |
| CW 297 | The Idea and Practice of the Waldorf School |
| CW 297a | Education for Life: Self-Education and the Practice of Pedagogy |
| CW 298 | Rudolf Steiner in the Waldorf School |
| CW 299 | Spiritual-Scientific Observations on Speech |
| CW 300a | Conferences with the Teachers of the Free Waldorf School in Stuttgart, 1919 to 1924, in 3 Volumes, Vol. 1 |
| CW 300b | Conferences with the Teachers of the Free Waldorf School in Stuttgart, 1919 to 1924, in 3 Volumes, Vol. 2 |
| CW 300c | Conferences with the Teachers of the Free Waldorf School in Stuttgart, 1919 to 1924, in 3 Volumes, Vol. 3 |
| CW 301 | The Renewal of Pedagogical-Didactical Art through Spiritual Science |
| CW 302 | Knowledge of the Human Being and the Forming of Class Lessons |
| CW 302a | Education and Teaching from a Knowledge of the Human Being |
| CW 303 | The Healthy Development of the Human Being |
| CW 304 | Methods of Education and Teaching Based on Anthroposophy |
| CW 304a | Anthroposophical Knowledge of the Human Being and Pedagogy |

# SIGNIFICANT EVENTS IN THE LIFE OF
## RUDOLF STEINER

1829:   June 23: birth of Johann Steiner (1829–1910)—Rudolf Steiner's father—in Geras, Lower Austria.

1834:   May 8: birth of Franciska Blie (1834–1918)—Rudolf Steiner's mother—in Horn, Lower Austria. 'My father and mother were both children of the glorious Lower Austrian forest district north of the Danube.'

1860:   May 16: marriage of Johann Steiner and Franciska Blie.

1861:   February 25: birth of *Rudolf Joseph Lorenz Steiner* in Kraljevec, Croatia, near the border with Hungary, where Johann Steiner works as a telegrapher for the South Austria Railroad. Rudolf Steiner is baptized two days later, February 27, the date usually given as his birthday.

1862:   Summer: the family moves to Modling, Lower Austria.

1863:   The family moves to Pottschach, Lower Austria, near the Styrian border, where Johann Steiner becomes stationmaster. 'The view stretched to the mountains . . . majestic peaks in the distance and the sweet charm of nature in the immediate surroundings.'

1864:   November 15: birth of Rudolf Steiner's sister, Leopoldine (d. November 1, 1927). She will become a seamstress and live with her parents for the rest of her life.

1866:   July 28: birth of Rudolf Steiner's deaf-mute brother, Gustav (d. May 1, 1941).

1867:   Rudolf Steiner enters the village school. Following a disagreement between his father and the schoolmaster, whose wife falsely accused the boy of causing a commotion, Rudolf Steiner is taken out of school and taught at home.

1868:   A critical experience. Unknown to the family, an aunt dies in a distant town. Sitting in the station waiting room, Rudolf Steiner sees her 'form,' which speaks to him, asking for help. 'Beginning with this experience, a new soul life began in the boy, one in which not only the outer trees and mountains spoke to him, but also the worlds that lay behind them. From this moment on, the boy began to live with the spirits of nature . . .'

1869: The family moves to the peaceful, rural village of Neudorfl, near Wiener Neustadt in present-day Austria. Rudolf Steiner attends the village school. Because of the 'unorthodoxy' of his writing and spelling, he has to do 'extra lessons'.

1870: Through a book lent to him by his tutor, he discovers geometry: 'To grasp something purely in the spirit brought me inner happiness. I know that I first learned happiness through geometry.' The same tutor allows him to draw, while other students still struggle with their reading and writing. 'An artistic element' thus enters his education.

1871: Though his parents are not religious, Rudolf Steiner becomes a 'church child,' a favourite of the priest, who was 'an exceptional character.' 'Up to the age of ten or eleven, among those I came to know, he was far and away the most significant.' Among other things, he introduces Steiner to Copernican, heliocentric cosmology. As an altar boy, Rudolf Steiner serves at Masses, funerals, and Corpus Christi processions. At year's end, after an incident in which he escapes a thrashing, his father forbids him to go to church.

1872: Rudolf Steiner transfers to grammar school in Wiener-Neustadt, a five-mile walk from home, which must be done in all weathers.

1873–75: Through his teachers and on his own, Rudolf Steiner has many wonderful experiences with science and mathematics. Outside school, he teaches himself analytic geometry, trigonometry, differential equations, and calculus.

1876: Rudolf Steiner begins tutoring other students. He learns bookbinding from his father. He also teaches himself stenography.

1877: Rudolf Steiner discovers Kant's *Critique of Pure Reason,* which he reads and rereads. He also discovers and reads von Rotteck's *World History.*

1878: He studies extensively in contemporary psychology and philosophy.

1879: Rudolf Steiner graduates from high school with honours. His father is transferred to Inzersdorf, near Vienna. He uses his first visit to Vienna 'to purchase a great number of philosophy books'—Kant, Fichte, Schelling, and Hegel, as well as numerous histories of philosophy. His aim: to find a path from the 'I' to nature.

October
1879–1883: Rudolf Steiner attends the Technical College in Vienna—to study mathematics, chemistry, physics, mineralogy, botany, zoology,

biology, geology, and mechanics—with a scholarship. He also attends lectures in history and literature, while avidly reading philosophy on his own. His two favourite professors are Karl Julius Schröer (German language and literature) and Edmund Reitlinger (physics). He also audits lectures by Robert Zimmermann on aesthetics and Franz Brentano on philosophy. During this year he begins his friendship with Moritz Zitter (1861–1921), who will help support him financially when he is in Berlin.

1880: Rudolf Steiner attends lectures on Schiller and Goethe by Karl Julius Schröer, who becomes his mentor. Also 'through a remarkable combination of circumstances,' he meets Felix Koguzki, a 'herb gatherer' and healer, who could 'see deeply into the secrets of nature'. Rudolf Steiner will meet and study with this 'emissary of the Master' throughout his time in Vienna.

1881: January: '... I didn't sleep a wink. I was busy with philosophical problems until about 12:30 a.m. Then, finally, I threw myself down on my couch. All my striving during the previous year had been to research whether the following statement by Schelling was true or not: *Within everyone dwells a secret, marvellous capacity to draw back from the stream of time—out of the self clothed in all that comes to us from outside—into our innermost being and there, in the immutable form of the Eternal, to look into ourselves.* I believe, and I am still quite certain of it, that I discovered this capacity in myself; I had long had an inkling of it. Now the whole of idealist philosophy stood before me in modified form. What's a sleepless night compared to that!'

Rudolf Steiner begins communicating with leading thinkers of the day, who send him books in return, which he reads eagerly.

July: 'I am not one of those who dives into the day like an animal in human form. I pursue a quite specific goal, an idealistic aim—knowledge of the truth! This cannot be done offhandedly. It requires the greatest striving in the world, free of all egotism, and equally of all resignation.'

August: Steiner puts down on paper for the first time thoughts for a 'Philosophy of Freedom.' 'The striving for the absolute: this human yearning is freedom.' He also seeks to outline a 'peasant philosophy,' describing what the worldview of a 'peasant'—one who lives close to the earth and the old ways—really is.

1881–1882: Felix Koguzki, the herb gatherer, reveals himself to be the envoy of another, higher initiatory personality, who instructs Rudolf Steiner to penetrate Fichte's philosophy and to master modern scientific thinking as a preparation for right entry into the spirit. This 'Master' also teaches him the double (evolutionary and involutionary) nature of time.

1882: Through the offices of Karl Julius Schröer, Rudolf Steiner is asked by Joseph Kürschner to edit Goethe's scientific works for the *Deutschen National-Literatur* edition. He writes 'A Possible Critique of Atomistic Concepts' and sends it to Friedrich Theodor Vischer.

1883: Rudolf Steiner completes his college studies and begins work on the Goethe project.

1884: First volume of Goethe's *Scientific Writings* (CW 1) appears (March). He lectures on Goethe and Lessing, and Goethe's approach to science. In July, he enters the household of Ladislaus and Pauline Specht as tutor to the four Specht boys. He will live there until 1890. At this time, he meets Josef Breuer (1842–1925), the co-author with Sigmund Freud of *Studies in Hysteria,* who is the Specht family doctor.

1885: While continuing to edit Goethe's writings, Rudolf Steiner reads deeply in contemporary philosophy (Eduard von Hartmann, Johannes Volkelt, and Richard Wahle, among others).

1886: May: Rudolf Steiner sends Kürschner the manuscript of *Outlines of Goethe's Theory of Knowledge* (CW 2), which appears in October, and which he sends out widely. He also meets the poet Marie Eugenie Delle Grazie and writes 'Nature and Our Ideals' for her. He attends her salon, where he meets many priests, theologians, and philosophers, who will become his friends. Meanwhile, the director of the Goethe Archive in Weimar requests his collaboration with the *Sophien* edition of Goethe's works, particularly the writings on colour.

1887: At the beginning of the year, Rudolf Steiner is very sick. As the year progresses and his health improves, he becomes increasingly 'a man of letters,' lecturing, writing essays, and taking part in Austrian cultural life. In August–September, the second volume of Goethe's *Scientific Writings* appears.

1888: January–July: Rudolf Steiner assumes editorship of the 'German Weekly' *(Deutsche Wochenschrift)*. He begins lecturing more intensively, giving, for example, a lecture titled 'Goethe as Father of a New Aesthetics.' He meets and becomes soul friends with Friedrich Eckstein (1861–1939), a vegetarian, philosopher of symbolism, alchemist, and musician, who will introduce him to various spiritual currents (including Theosophy) and with whom he will meditate and interpret esoteric and alchemical texts.

1889: Rudolf Steiner first reads Nietzsche *(Beyond Good and Evil)*. He encounters Theosophy again and learns of Madame Blavatsky in the theosophical circle around Marie Lang (1858–1934). Here he also meets well-known figures of Austrian life, as well as esoteric figures like the occultist Franz Hartmann and Karl Leinigen-Billigen (translator of C.G. Harrison's *The Transcendental Universe*). During this period, Steiner first reads A.P. Sinnett's *Esoteric Buddhism* and Mabel Collins's *Light on the Path*. He also begins travelling, visiting Budapest, Weimar, and Berlin (where he meets philosopher Eduard von Hartmann).

1890:      Rudolf Steiner finishes Volume 3 of Goethe's scientific writings. He begins his doctoral dissertation, which will become *Truth and Science* (CW 3). He also meets the poet and feminist Rosa Mayreder (1858–1938), with whom he can exchange his most intimate thoughts. In September, Rudolf Steiner moves to Weimar to work in the Goethe-Schiller Archive.

1891:      Volume 3 of the Kürschner edition of Goethe appears. Meanwhile, Rudolf Steiner edits Goethe's studies in mineralogy and scientific writings for the *Sophien* edition. He meets Ludwig Laistner of the Cotta Publishing Company, who asks for a book on the basic question of metaphysics. From this will result, ultimately, *The Philosophy of Freedom* (CW 4), which will be published not by Cotta but by Emil Felber. In October, Rudolf Steiner takes the oral exam for a doctorate in philosophy, mathematics, and mechanics at Rostock University, receiving his doctorate on the twenty-sixth. In November, he gives his first lecture on Goethe's 'Fairy Tale' in Vienna.

1892:      Rudolf Steiner continues work at the Goethe-Schiller Archive and on his *Philosophy of Freedom*. *Truth and Science,* his doctoral dissertation, is published. Steiner undertakes to write Introductions to books on Schopenhauer and Jean Paul for Cotta. At year's end, he finds lodging with Anna Eunike, née Schulz (1853–1911), a widow with four daughters and a son. He also develops a friendship with Otto Erich Hartleben (1864–1905) with whom he shares literary interests.

1893:      Rudolf Steiner begins his habit of producing many reviews and articles. In March, he gives a lecture titled 'Hypnotism, with Reference to Spiritism.' In September, volume 4 of the Kürschner edition is completed. In November, *The Philosophy of Freedom* appears. This year, too, he meets John Henry Mackay (1864–1933), the anarchist, and Max Stirner, a scholar and biographer.

1894:      Rudolf Steiner meets Elisabeth Fürster Nietzsche, the philosopher's sister, and begins to read Nietzsche in earnest, beginning with the as yet unpublished *Antichrist*. He also meets Ernst Haeckel (1834–1919). In the fall, he begins to write *Nietzsche, A Fighter against His Time* (CW 5).

1895:      May, *Nietzsche, A Fighter against His Time* appears.

1896:      January 22: Rudolf Steiner sees Friedrich Nietzsche for the first and only time. Moves between the Nietzsche and the Goethe-Schiller

Archives, where he completes his work before year's end. He falls out with Elisabeth Förster Nietzsche, thus ending his association with the Nietzsche Archive.

1897: Rudolf Steiner finishes the manuscript of *Goethe's Worldview* (CW 6). He moves to Berlin with Anna Eunike and begins editorship of the *Magazin für Literatur*. From now on, Steiner will write countless reviews, literary and philosophical articles, and so on. He begins lecturing at the 'Free Literary Society.' In September, he attends the Zionist Congress in Basel. He sides with Dreyfus in the Dreyfus affair.

1898: Rudolf Steiner is very active as an editor in the political, artistic, and theatrical life of Berlin. He becomes friendly with John Henry Mackay and poet Ludwig Jacobowski (1868–1900). He joins Jacobowski's circle of writers, artists, and scientists—'The Coming Ones' (*Die Kommenden*)—and contributes lectures to the group until 1903. He also lectures at the 'League for College Pedagogy.' He writes an article for Goethe's sesquicentennial, 'Goethe's Secret Revelation,' on the 'Fairy Tale of the Green Snake and the Beautiful Lily.'

1898–99: 'This was a trying time for my soul as I looked at Christianity. . . . I was able to progress only by contemplating, by means of spiritual perception, the evolution of Christianity. . . . Conscious knowledge of real Christianity began to dawn in me around the turn of the century. This seed continued to develop. My soul trial occurred shortly before the beginning of the twentieth century. It was decisive for my soul's development that I stood spiritually before the Mystery of Golgotha in a deep and solemn celebration of knowledge.'

1899: Rudolf Steiner begins teaching and giving lectures and lecture cycles at the Workers' College, founded by Wilhelm Liebknecht (1826–1900). He will continue to do so until 1904. Writes: *Literature and Spiritual Life in the Nineteenth Century; Individualism in Philosophy; Haeckel and His Opponents; Poetry in the Present;* and begins what will become (fifteen years later) *The Riddles of Philosophy* (CW 18). He also meets many artists and writers, including Käthe Kollwitz, Stefan Zweig, and Rainer Maria Rilke. On October 31, he marries Anna Eunike.

1900: 'I thought that the turn of the century must bring humanity a new light. It seemed to me that the separation of human thinking and willing from the spirit had peaked. A turn or reversal of direction in human evolution seemed to me a necessity.' Rudolf Steiner finishes *World and Life Views in the Nineteenth Century* (the second part of what will become *The Riddles of Philosophy*) and dedicates it to

Ernst Haeckel. It is published in March. He continues lecturing at *Die Kommenden,* whose leadership he assumes after the death of Jacobowski. Also, he gives the Gutenberg Jubilee lecture before 7,000 typesetters and printers. In September, Rudolf Steiner is invited by Count and Countess Brockdorff to lecture in the Theosophical Library. His first lecture is on Nietzsche. His second lecture is titled 'Goethe's Secret Revelation.' October 6, he begins a lecture cycle on the mystics that will become *Mystics after Modernism* (CW 7). November–December: 'Marie von Sivers appears in the audience. . . .' Also in November, Steiner gives his first lecture at the Giordano Bruno Bund (where he will continue to lecture until May, 1905). He speaks on Bruno and modern Rome, focusing on the importance of the philosophy of Thomas Aquinas as monism.

1901:    In continual financial straits, Rudolf Steiner's early friends Moritz Zitter and Rosa Mayreder help support him. In October, he begins the lecture cycle *Christianity as Mystical Fact* (CW 8) at the Theosophical Library. In November, he gives his first 'theosophical lecture' on Goethe's 'Fairy Tale' in Hamburg at the invitation of Wilhelm Hubbe-Schleiden. He also attends a gathering to celebrate the founding of the Theosophical Society at Count and Countess Brockdorff's. He gives a lecture cycle, 'From Buddha to Christ,' for the circle of the *Kommenden.* November 17, Marie von Sivers asks Rudolf Steiner if Theosophy needs a Western–Christian spiritual movement (to complement Theosophy's Eastern emphasis). 'The question was posed. Now, following spiritual laws, I could begin to give an answer. . . .' In December, Rudolf Steiner writes his first article for a theosophical publication. At year's end, the Brockdorffs and possibly Wilhelm Hubbe-Schleiden ask Rudolf Steiner to join the Theosophical Society and undertake the leadership of the German section. Rudolf Steiner agrees, on the condition that Marie von Sivers (then in Italy) work with him.

1902:    Beginning in January, Rudolf Steiner attends the opening of the Workers' School in Spandau with Rosa Luxemburg (1870–1919). January 17, Rudolf Steiner joins the Theosophical Society. In April, he is asked to become general secretary of the German Section of the theosophical Society, and works on preparations for its founding. In July, he visits London for a theosophical congress. He meets Bertram Keightly, G.R.S. Mead, A.P. Sinnett, and Annie Besant, among others. In September, *Christianity as Mystical Fact* appears. In October, Rudolf Steiner gives his first public lecture on Theosophy ('Monism and Theosophy') to about three hundred people at the Giordano Bruno Bund. On October 19–21, the

German Section of the Theosophical Society has its first meeting; Rudolf Steiner is the general secretary, and Annie Besant attends. Steiner lectures on practical karma studies. On October 23, Annie Besant inducts Rudolf Steiner into the Esoteric School of the Theosophical Society. On October 25, Steiner begins a weekly series of lectures: 'The Field of Theosophy.' During this year, Rudolf Steiner also first meets Ita Wegman (1876–1943), who will become his close collaborator in his final years.

1903: Rudolf Steiner holds about 300 lectures and seminars. In May, the first issue of the periodical *Luzifer* appears. In June, Rudolf Steiner visits London for the first meeting of the Federation of the European Sections of the Theosophical Society, where he meets Colonel Olcott. He begins to write *Theosophy* (CW 9).

1904: Rudolf Steiner continues lecturing at the Workers' College and elsewhere (about 90 lectures), while lecturing intensively all over Germany among theosophists (about 140 lectures). In February, he meets Carl Unger (1878–1929), who will become a member of the board of the Anthroposophical Society (1913). In March, he meets Michael Bauer (1871–1929), a Christian mystic, who will also be on the board. In May, *Theosophy* appears, with the dedication: 'To the spirit of Giordano Bruno.' Rudolf Steiner and Marie von Sivers visit London for meetings with Annie Besant. June: Rudolf Steiner and Marie von Sivers attend the meeting of the Federation of European Sections of the Theosophical Society in Amsterdam. In July, Steiner begins the articles in *Luzifer-Gnosis* that will become *How to Know Higher Worlds* (CW 10) and *Cosmic Memory* (CW 11). In September, Annie Besant visits Germany. In December, Steiner lectures on Freemasonry. He mentions the High Grade Masonry derived from John Yarker and represented by Theodore Reuss and Karl Kellner as a blank slate 'into which a good image could be placed'.

1905: This year, Steiner ends his non-theosophical lecturing activity. Supported by Marie von Sivers, his theosophical lecturing—both in public and in the Theosophical Society—increases significantly: 'The German Theosophical Movement is of exceptional importance.' Steiner recommends reading, among others, Fichte, Jacob Boehme, and Angelus Silesius. He begins to introduce Christian themes into Theosophy. He also begins to work with doctors (Felix Peipers and Ludwig Noll). In July, he is in London for the Federation of European Sections, where he attends a lecture by Annie Besant: 'I have seldom seen Mrs Besant speak in so inward and heartfelt a manner... Through Mrs Besant I have found the way to H.P. Blavatsky.' September to October, hc gives a course of 31 lectures for a small group of esoteric students. In October, the annual meeting of the German Section of the Theosophical Society, which still remains very small, takes place. Rudolf Steiner reports membership has risen from 121 to 377 members. In November, seeking to establish esoteric 'continuity,' Rudolf Steiner and Marie von Sivers participate in a 'Memphis-Misraim' Masonic ceremony. They pay 45 marks for membership. 'Yesterday, you saw how little remains of former esoteric institutions.' 'We are dealing only with a "framework" … for the present, nothing lies behind it. The occult powers have completely withdrawn.'

1906:     Expansion of theosophical work. Rudolf Steiner gives about 245 lectures, only 44 of which take place in Berlin. Cycles are given in Paris, Leipzig, Stuttgart, and Munich. Esoteric work also intensifies. Rudolf Steiner begins writing *An Outline of Esoteric Science* (CW 13). In January, Rudolf Steiner receives permission (a patent) from the Great Orient of the Scottish A & A Thirty-Three Degree Rite of the Order of the Ancient Freemasons of the Memphis-Misraim Rite to direct a chapter under the name 'Mystica Aeterna.' This will become the 'Cognitive-Ritual Section' (also called 'Misraim Service') of the Esoteric School. (See: *Freemasonry and Ritual Work: The Misraim Service*, CW 265.) During this time, Steiner also meets Albert Schweitzer. In May, he is in Paris, where he visits Édouard Schuré. Many Russians attend his lectures (including Konstantin Balmont, Dimitri Mereszkovski, Zinaida Hippius, and Maximilian Woloshin). He attends the General Meeting of the European Federation of the Theosophical Society, at which Col Olcott is present for the last time. He spends the year's end in Venice and Rome, where he writes and works on his translation of H.P. Blavatsky's *Key to Theosophy*.

1907:     Further expansion of the German Theosophical Movement according to the Rosicrucian directive to 'introduce spirit into the world'—in education, in social questions, in art, and in science. In February, Col Olcott dies in Adyar. Before he dies, Olcott indicates that 'the Masters' wish Annie Besant to succeed him: much politicking ensues. Rudolf Steiner supports Besant's candidacy. April–May: preparations for the Congress of the Federation of European Sections of the Theosophical Society—the great, watershed Whitsun 'Munich Congress,' attended by Annie Besant and others. Steiner decides to separate Eastern and Western (Christian–Rosicrucian) esoteric schools. He takes his esoteric school out of the Theosophical Society (Besant and Rudolf Steiner are 'in harmony' on this). Steiner makes his first lecture tours to Austria and Hungary. That summer, he is in Italy. In September, he visits Édouard Schuré, who will write the Introduction to the French edition of *Christianity as Mystical Fact* in Barr, Alsace. Rudolf Steiner writes the autobiographical statement known as the 'Barr Document.' In *Luzifer-Gnosis*, 'The Education of the Child' appears.

1908:    The movement grows (membership: 1,150). Lecturing expands. Steiner makes his first extended lecture tour to Holland and Scandinavia, as well as visits to Naples and Sicily. Themes: St John's Gospel, the Apocalypse, Egypt, science, philosophy, and logic. *Luzifer-Gnosis* ceases publication. In Berlin, Marie von Sivers (with Johanna Mücke (1864–1949) forms the *Philosophisch-Theosophisch* (after 1915 *Philosophisch-Anthroposophisch) Verlag* to publish Steiner's work. Steiner gives lecture cycles titled *The Gospel of St John* (CW 103) and *The Apocalypse* (104).

1909:    *An Outline of Esoteric Science* appears. Lecturing and travel continues. Rudolf Steiner's spiritual research expands to include the polarity of Lucifer and Ahriman; the work of great individualities in history; the Maitreya Buddha and the Bodhisattvas; spiritual economy (CW 109); the work of the spiritual hierarchies in heaven and on earth (CW 110). He also deepens and intensifies his research into the Gospels, giving lectures on the Gospel of St Luke (CW 114) with the first mention of two Jesus children. Meets and becomes friends with Christian Morgenstern (1871–1914). In April, he lays the foundation stone for the Malsch model—the building that will lead to the first Goetheanum. In May, the International Congress of the Federation of European Sections of the Theosophical Society takes place in Budapest. Rudolf Steiner receives the Subba Row medal for *How to Know Higher Worlds*. During this time, Charles W. Leadbeater discovers Jiddu Krishnamurti (1895–1986) and proclaims him the future 'world teacher,' the bearer of the Maitreya Buddha and the 'reappearing Christ.' In October, Steiner delivers seminal lectures on 'anthroposophy,' which he will try, unsuccessfully, to rework over the next years into the unfinished work, *Anthroposophy (A Fragment)* (CW 45).

1910:    New themes: *The Reappearance of Christ in the Etheric* (CW 118); *The Fifth Gospel; The Mission of Folk Souls* (CW 121); *Occult History* (CW 126); the evolving development of etheric cognitive capacities. Rudolf Steiner continues his Gospel research with *The Gospel of St Matthew* (CW 123). In January, his father dies. In April, he takes a month-long trip to Italy, including Rome, Monte Cassino, and Sicily. He also visits Scandinavia again. July–August, he writes the first Mystery Drama, *The Portal of Initiation* (CW 14). In November, he gives 'psychosophy' lectures. In December, he submits 'On the

**1911:**  Psychological Foundations and Epistemological Framework of Theosophy' to the International Philosophical Congress in Bologna. The crisis in the Theosophical Society deepens. In January, 'The Order of the Rising Sun,' which will soon become 'The Order of the Star in the East,' is founded for the coming world teacher, Krishnamurti. At the same time, Marie von Sivers, Rudolf Steiner's co-worker, falls ill. Fewer lectures are given, but important new ground is broken. In Prague, in March, Steiner meets Franz Kafka (1883–1924) and Hugo Bergmann (1883–1975). In April, he delivers his paper to the Philosophical Congress. He writes the second Mystery Drama, *The Soul's Probation* (CW 14). Also, while Marie von Sivers is convalescing, Rudolf Steiner begins work on *Calendar 1912/1913*, which will contain the 'Calendar of the Soul' meditations. On March 19, Anna (Eunike) Steiner dies. In September, Rudolf Steiner visits Einsiedeln, birthplace of Paracelsus. In December, Friedrich Rittelmeyer, future founder of the Christian Community, meets Rudolf Steiner. The *Johannes-Bauverein*, the 'building committee,' which would lead to the first Goetheanum (first planned for Munich), is also founded, and a preliminary committee for the founding of an independent association is created that, in the following year, will become the Anthroposophical Society. Important lecture cycles include *Occult Physiology* (CW 128); *Wonders of the World* (CW 129); *From Jesus to Christ* (CW 131). Other themes: esoteric Christianity; Christian Rosenkreutz; the spiritual guidance of humanity; the sense world and the world of the spirit.

**1912:**  Despite the ongoing, now increasing crisis in the Theosophical Society, much is accomplished: *Calendar 1912/1913* is published; eurythmy is created; both the third Mystery Drama, *The Guardian of the Threshold* (CW 14) and *A Way of Self-Knowledge* (CW 16) are written. New (or renewed) themes included life between death and rebirth and karma and reincarnation. Other lecture cycles: *Spiritual Beings in the Heavenly Bodies and in the Kingdoms of Nature* (CW 136); *The Human Being in the Light of Occultism, Theosophy, and Philosophy* (CW 137); *The Gospel of St Mark* (CW 139); and *The Bhagavad Gita and the Epistles of Paul* (CW 142). On May 8, Rudolf Steiner celebrates White Lotus Day, H.P. Blavatsky's death day, which he had faithfully observed for the past decade, for the last time. In August, Rudolf Steiner suggests the 'independent association' be called the 'Anthroposophical Society.' In September, the first eurythmy course takes place. In October, Rudolf Steiner declines recognition of a Theosophical Society lodge dedicated to the Star of the East and decides to expel all Theosophical Society members belonging to the order.

Also, with Marie von Sivers, he first visits Dornach, near Basel, Switzerland, and they stand on the hill where the Goetheanum will be built. In November, a Theosophical Society lodge is opened by direct mandate from Adyar (Annie Besant). In December, a meeting of the German section occurs at which it is decided that belonging to the Order of the Star of the East is incompatible with membership in the Theosophical Society. December 28: informal founding of the Anthroposophical Society in Berlin.

1913:    Expulsion of the German section from the Theosophical Society. February 2–3: Foundation meeting of the Anthroposophical Society. Board members include: Marie von Sivers, Michael Bauer, and Carl Unger. September 20: Laying of the foundation stone for the *Johannes Bau* (Goetheanum) in Dornach. Building begins immediately. The fourth Mystery Drama, *The Soul's Awakening* (CW 14), is completed. Also: *The Threshold of the Spiritual World* (CW 147). Lecture cycles include: *The Bhagavad Gita and the Epistles of Paul* and *The Esoteric Meaning of the Bhagavad Gita* (CW 146), which the Russian philosopher Nikolai Berdyaev attends; *The Mysteries of the East and of Christianity* (CW 144); *The Effects of Esoteric Development* (CW 145); and *The Fifth Gospel* (CW 148). In May, Rudolf Steiner is in London and Paris, where anthroposophical work continues.

1914:    Building continues on the *Johannes Bau* (Goetheanum) in Dornach, with artists and co-workers from seventeen nations. The general assembly of the Anthroposophical Society takes place. In May, Rudolf Steiner visits Paris, as well as Chartres Cathedral. June 28: assassination in Sarajevo ('Now the catastrophe has happened!'). August 1: War is declared. Rudolf Steiner returns to Germany from Dornach—he will travel back and forth. He writes the last chapter of *The Riddles of Philosophy*. Lecture cycles include: *Human and Cosmic Thought* (CW 151); *Inner Being of Humanity between Death and a New Birth* (CW 153); *Occult Reading and Occult Hearing* (CW 156). December 24: marriage of Rudolf Steiner and Marie von Sivers.

1915:    Building continues. Life after death becomes a major theme, also art. Writes: *Thoughts during a Time of War* (CW 24). Lectures include: *The Secret of Death* (CW 159); *The Uniting of Humanity through the Christ Impulse* (CW 165).

1916:    Rudolf Steiner begins work with Edith Maryon (1872–1924) on the sculpture 'The Representative of Humanity' ('The Group'— Christ, Lucifer, and Ahriman). He also works with the alchemist Alexander von Bernus on the quarterly *Das Reich*. He writes *The Riddle of Humanity* (CW 20). Lectures include: *Necessity and Freedom in World History and Human Action* (CW 166); *Past and Present in the*

*Human Spirit* (CW 167); *The Karma of Vocation* (CW 172); *The Karma of Untruthfulness* (CW 173).

1917:  Russian Revolution. The U.S. enters the war. Building continues. Rudolf Steiner delineates the idea of the 'threefold nature of the human being' (in a public lecture March 15) and the 'threefold nature of the social organism' (hammered out in May–June with the help of Otto von Lerchenfeld and Ludwig Polzer-Hoditz in the form of two documents titled *Memoranda*, which were distributed in high places). August–September: Rudolf Steiner writes *The Riddles of the Soul* (CW 20). Also: commentary on 'The Chymical Wedding of Christian Rosenkreutz' for Alexander Bernus (*Das Reich*). Lectures include: *The Karma of Materialism* (CW 176); *The Spiritual Background of the Outer World: The Fall of the Spirits of Darkness* (CW 177).

1918:  March 18: peace treaty of Brest-Litovsk—'Now everything will truly enter chaos! What is needed is cultural renewal.' June: Rudolf Steiner visits Karlstein (Grail) Castle outside Prague. Lecture cycle: *From Symptom to Reality in Modern History* (CW 185). In mid-November, Emil Molt, of the Waldorf-Astoria Cigarette Company, has the idea of founding a school for his workers' children.

1919:  Focus on the threefold social organism: tireless travel, countless lectures, meetings, and publications. At the same time, a new public stage of Anthroposophy emerges as cultural renewal begins. The coming years will see initiatives in pedagogy, medicine, pharmacology, and agriculture. January 27: threefold meeting: 'We must first of all, with the money we have, found free schools that can bring people what they need.' February: first public eurythmy performance in Zurich. Also: 'Appeal to the German People' (CW 24), circulated March 6 as a newspaper insert. In April, *Towards Social Renewal* (CW 23) appears—'perhaps the most widely read of all books on politics appearing since the war'. Rudolf Steiner is asked to undertake the 'direction and leadership' of the school founded by the Waldorf-Astoria Company. Rudolf Steiner begins to talk about the 'renewal' of education. May 30: a building is selected and purchased for the future Waldorf School. August–September, Rudolf Steiner gives a lecture course for Waldorf teachers, *The Foundations of Human Experience (Study of Man)* (CW 293). September 7: Opening of the first Waldorf School. December (into January): first science course, the *Light Course* (CW 320).

1920:  The Waldorf School flourishes. New threefold initiatives. Founding of limited companies *Der Kommende Tag* and *Futurum A.G.* to infuse spiritual values into the economic realm. Rudolf Steiner also focuses on the sciences. Lectures: *Introducing Anthroposophical*

*Medicine* (CW 312); *The Warmth Course* (CW 321); *The Boundaries of Natural Science* (CW 322); *The Redemption of Thinking* (CW 74). February: Johannes Werner Klein—later a co-founder of The Christian Community—asks Rudolf Steiner about the possibility of a 'religious renewal,' a 'Johannine church.' In March, Rudolf Steiner gives the first course for doctors and medical students. In April, a divinity student asks Rudolf Steiner a second time about the possibility of religious renewal. September 27–October 16: anthroposophical 'university course.' December: lectures titled *The Search for the New Isis* (CW 202).

1921:　Rudolf Steiner continues his intensive work on cultural renewal, including the uphill battle for the threefold social order. 'University' arts, scientific, theological, and medical courses include: *The Astronomy Course* (CW 323); *Observation, Mathematics, and Scientific Experiment* (CW 324); the *Second Medical Course* (CW 313); *Colour.* In June and September–October, Rudolf Steiner also gives the first two 'priests' courses' (CW 342 and 343). The 'youth movement' gains momentum. Magazines are founded: *Die Drei* (January), and—under the editorship of Albert Steffen (1884–1963)—the weekly, *Das Goetheanum* (August). In February–March, Rudolf Steiner takes his first trip outside Germany since the war (Holland). On April 7, Steiner receives a letter regarding 'religious renewal,' and May 22–23, he agrees to address the question in a practical way. In June, the Klinical-Therapeutic Institute opens in Arlesheim under the direction of Dr Ita Wegman. In August, the Chemical-Pharmaceutical Laboratory opens in Arlesheim (Oskar Schmiedel and Ita Wegman are directors). The Clinical Therapeutic Institute is inaugurated in Stuttgart (Dr Ludwig Noll is director); also the Research Laboratory in Dornach (Ehrenfried Pfeiffer and Gunther Wachsmuth are directors). In November–December, Rudolf Steiner visits Norway.

1922:　The first half of the year involves very active public lecturing (thousands attend); in the second half, Rudolf Steiner begins to withdraw and turn toward the Society—'The Society is asleep.' It is 'too weak' to do what is asked of it. The businesses—*Der Kommende Tag* and *Futurum A.G.*—fail. In January, with the help of an agent, Steiner undertakes a twelve-city German lecture tour, accompanied by eurythmy performances. In two weeks he speaks to more than 2,000 people. In April, he gives a 'university course' in The Hague. He also visits England. In June, he is in Vienna for the East–West Congress. In August–September, he is back in England for the Oxford Conference on Education. Returning to Dornach, he gives the lectures *Philosophy, Cosmology, and Religion*

(CW 215), and gives the third priests' course (CW 344). On September 16, The Christian Community is founded. In October–November, Steiner is in Holland and England. He also speaks to the youth: *The Youth Course* (CW 217). In December, Steiner gives lectures titled *The Origins of Natural Science* (CW 326), and *Humanity and the World of Stars: The Spiritual Communion of Humanity* (CW 219). December 31: Fire at the Goetheanum, which is destroyed.

1923: Despite the fire, Rudolf Steiner continues his work unabated. A very hard year. Internal dispersion, dissension, and apathy abound. There is conflict—between old and new visions—within the Society. A wake-up call is needed, and Rudolf Steiner responds with renewed lecturing vitality. His focus: the spiritual context of human life; initiation science; the course of the year; and community building. As a foundation for an artistic school, he creates a series of pastel sketches. Lecture cycles: *The Anthroposophical Movement; Initiation Science* (CW 227) (in Wales at the Penmaenmawr Summer School); *The Four Seasons and the Archangels* (CW 229); *Harmony of the Creative Word* (CW 230); *The Supersensible Human* (CW 231), given in Holland for the founding of the Dutch Society. On November 10, in response to the failed Hitler-Ludendorff putsch in Munich, Steiner closes his Berlin residence and moves the *Philosophisch-Anthroposophisch Verlag* (Press) to Dornach. On December 9, Steiner begins the serialization of his *Autobiography: The Course of My Life* (CW 28) in *Das Goetheanum*. It will continue to appear weekly, without a break, until his death. Late December–early January: Rudolf Steiner re-founds the Anthroposophical Society (about 12,000 members internationally) and takes over its leadership. The new board members are: Marie Steiner, Ita Wegman, Albert Steffen, Elisabeth Vreede, and Gunther Wachsmuth. (See *The Christmas Meeting for the Founding of the General Anthroposophical Society*, CW 260.) Accompanying lectures: *Mystery Knowledge and Mystery Centres* (CW 232); *World History in the Light of Anthroposophy* (CW 233). December 25: the Foundation Stone is laid (in the hearts of members) in the form of the 'Foundation Stone Meditation.'

1924: January 1: having founded the Anthroposophical Society and taken over its leadership, Rudolf Steiner has the task of 'reforming' it. The process begins with a weekly newssheet ('What's Happening in the Anthroposophical Society') in which Rudolf Steiner's 'Letters to Members' and 'Anthroposophical Leading Thoughts' appear (CW 26). The next step is the creation of a new esoteric class, the 'first class' of the 'University of Spiritual Science' (which was to have been followed, had Rudolf Steiner lived longer, by two more advanced classes). Then comes a new language for

Anthroposophy—practical, phenomenological, and direct; and Rudolf Steiner creates the model for the second Goetheanum. He begins the series of extensive 'karma' lectures (CW 235–40); and finally, responding to needs, he creates two new initiatives: biodynamic agriculture and curative education. After the middle of the year, rumours begin to circulate regarding Steiner's health. Lectures: January–February, *Anthroposophy* (CW 234); February: *Tone Eurythmy* (CW 278); June: *The Agriculture Course* (CW 327); June–July: *Speech Eurythmy* (CW 279); *Curative Education* (CW 317); August: (England, 'Second International Summer School'), *Initiation Consciousness: True and False Paths in Spiritual Investigation* (CW 243); September: *Pastoral Medicine* (CW 318). On September 26, for the first time, Rudolf Steiner cancels a lecture. On September 28, he gives his last lecture. On September 29, he withdraws to his studio in the carpenter's shop; now he is definitively ill. Cared for by Ita Wegman, he continues working, however, and writing the weekly installments of his *Autobiography* and *Letters to the Members/ Leading Thoughts* (CW 26).

1925:   Rudolf Steiner, while continuing to work, continues to weaken. He finishes *Extending Practical Medicine* (CW 27) with Ita Wegman. On March 30, around ten in the morning, Rudolf Steiner dies.

# INDEX

phenomenon of, 34
physical and, 43
spiritual movement, 66, 76, 110
  conditions for, 78
  genuine, 79
  intervention of, 39
  modern, 98
  purely, 77
spiritual realm, 21–22, 30
  reality in, 75
spiritual society, 92–93
spiritual world, 3–4, 7, 12, 14,
    22, 26, 32–33, 35, 37, 50, 53,
    55, 59–60, 62–63, 68, 72, 87,
    115–116, 129–130
  birth in, 65
  depiction of, 52
  discovery of, 71
  existence of, 11
  experience of, 8, 48
  human soul and, 96
  knowledge of, 65
  language of, 58
  real, 31, 78, 125
  revelation of, 12, 36, 49
  and spiritual methodology,
    112
Steiner, Marie, 102, 109
Steiner, Rudolf
  *The Philosophy of Freedom*,
    21–22, 107, 115, 120–122,
    129
  *Theory of Knowledge*, 116
Stifter, Adalbert, 38, 50
Strauß, David Friedrich,
    123
Stuttgart, 85, 88, 92

**T**

theosophical movement, 16, 67,
    77, 79–82, 85, 89, 93
Theosophical Society, 14, 16–18,
    22, 35, 53–54, 72, 77, 81,
    84–88, 94–96, 101, 108, 125
  absurdities of, 76
  access to, 79
  congress of, 80
  Dutch Section of, 75
  German Section of, 28
  leaders of, 73, 75, 93
  members of, 21, 23, 74
  purpose of, 83
  representative of, 20
  traditions of, 74
theosophy, 12, 15–17, 24, 26, 28,
    53–54, 83, 88, 125
  anthroposophy and, 80
  doctrines of, 18
  dogmas of, 29
  and imperialism, 78
truth, 21, 31, 40, 47, 57, 108, 116
  ancient, 12
  anthropological, 26
  Christian, 59
  cosmic, 90
  criterion of, 70
  devoid of, 102
  eternal, 119
  great, 13
  human, 90
  pure, 119
  and reality, 130
  spiritual, 60
  wisdom and, 99

## A NOTE FROM RUDOLF STEINER PRESS

We are an independent publisher and registered charity (non-profit organisation) dedicated to making available the work of Rudolf Steiner in English translation. We care a great deal about the content of our books and have hundreds of titles available – as printed books, ebooks and in audio formats.

### As a publisher devoted to anthroposophy...

- We continually commission translations of previously unpublished works by Rudolf Steiner and invest in updating, editing and improving our editions.

- We are committed to making anthroposophy available to all by publishing introductory books as well as contemporary research.

- Our new print editions and ebooks are carefully checked and proofread for accuracy, and converted into all formats for all platforms.

- Our translations are officially authorised by Rudolf Steiner's estate in Dornach, Switzerland, to whom we pay royalties on sales, thus assisting their critical work.

So, look out for Rudolf Steiner Press as a mark of quality and support us today by buying our books, or contact us should you wish to sponsor specific titles or to support the charity with a gift or legacy.

office@rudolfsteinerpress.com
Join our e-mailing list at www.rudolfsteinerpress.com

### RUDOLF STEINER PRESS